How Superstore Sprawl Can Harm Communities

And what citizens can do about it

by
Constance E. Beaumont

with a Preface by
Richard Moe

**National Trust for
Historic Preservation**

This publication was produced by the National Trust for Historic Preservation, a private nonprofit organization with more than 250,000 members dedicated to protecting the nation's cultural heritage. The Trust was chartered by Congress in 1949.

The mission of the National Trust for Historic Preservation is to foster an appreciation of the diverse character and meaning of our American cultural heritage and to preserve and revitalize the livability of our communities by leading the nation in saving America's historic environments.

For more information on the National Trust, call (202) 588-6000, or write the NTHP at 1785 Massachusetts Avenue, N.W., Washington, D.C. 20036

2nd Printing
ISBN 0-89133-392-4

Book design by John M. Lavery
Production by She Can Do It

(Cover Photo: Catherine Karnow; Woodfin Camp, Inc.)

Dedication

The National Trust for Historic Preservation respectfully dedicates this citizen's guide to the memory of George W. Dean (1930-1993) of Chestertown, Maryland. In a distinguished legal career spanning four decades, George Dean was a tireless advocate for the public interest as well as a preservationist of the highest order. During the last years of his life, he completed the restoration of three important historic properties, including the principal hotel on Chestertown's main street. He also provided inspiration and leadership to a group of fellow citizens determined to resist the intrusion of a huge superstore on the outskirts of Chestertown. This publication was made possible in part by contributions from George Dean's friends in his memory.

Acknowledgements

Many people contributed to this publication.

I wish particularly to thank Richard Moe, president of the National Trust for Historic Preservation, whose encouragement, guidance and leadership all played a critical role in the development of this citizen's guide.

Colleagues at the National Trust who were especially generous with their time in reviewing and commenting on early drafts include Dwight Young, Peter Brink, Alexandra Acosta, Julia Miller and Bridget Hartman. Elizabeth L. Wainger and Kennedy Smith contributed entire chapters—on media strategies and downtown revitalization, respectively. Laura Skaggs offered much helpful advice, while Kirsten Peeler worked hard to gather photographs and illustrations.

Others at the Trust whom I wish to thank for their help and cooperation are Vin Cipolla, Linda Cohen, Courtney Damkroger, David Doheny, Paul Edmondson, Jim Lindberg, Shelley Mastran, Elizabeth Merritt, Leilah Powell, Laurie Rabe, Andrea Sanford, Nancy Sizer, Libby Willis and Claudia Wu.

People outside the Trust contributed as well. Edward T. McMahon encouraged us to focus on the issue of superstore sprawl in the first place. Paul Bruhn offered much valued encouragement and many thoughtful suggestions. Citizen activists—notably Elizabeth Michaud, Emily Teller, Al Norman, Steve Alves and Cynthia Heslen—responded helpfully to many calls and questions. Frank C. Frantz and Harry K. Schwartz reviewed early drafts and recommended numerous improvements. Finally, Greg Holcombe, Caleb Faux, Marcia Smith, Chris Rigby, Jan Teehan, Julian Price, Elaine Bergman and Dana Beach were especially helpful in gathering photographs.

— Constance E. Beaumont

Contents

Part Three:
Case Studies and Better Models

Preface

One spring day in Mississippi, William Faulkner fired off a letter to his hometown paper, the *Oxford Eagle*. Outraged over a proposal to demolish Oxford's historic courthouse, Faulkner recalled another landmark torn down several years earlier:

It was tougher than war, tougher than the Yankee Brigadier Chalmers and his artillery and all his sappers with dynamite and crowbars and cans of kerosene. But it wasn't tougher than the ringing of a cash register bell. It had to go — obliterated, effaced, no trace left — so that a sprawling octopus covering the country from Portland, Maine to Oregon can dispense in cut-rate bargain lots, bananas and toilet paper.

They call this progress. But they don't say where it's going; also there are some of us who would like the chance to say whether or not we want the ride.

Though written in 1947, these words have a distinctly contemporary ring. They characterize the way many people feel today about the effects of modern superstores on the American landscape. As Gene Davidson, a resident of Berea, Ohio, wrote in a letter to me:

I believe that the "land that we love" is literally vanishing before our eyes. The present new construction rate of Wal-Mart, Super Kmarts, Meijers, and others of the "superstore" breed guarantees an inevitable destruction of much of what we hold dear. Add to the new construction starts of the superstores all of the franchise operations, such as Sub-Way, McDonalds, Taco Bell, etc., and you can project ten years down the road an intolerable situation. This country would eventually be virtually unrecognizable from what we knew as the United States just one generation ago.

The American retailing industry entered a new phase at some point during the last decade. Whereas the sixties and seventies had witnessed a proliferation of regional shopping malls in the suburbs, the late eighties and nineties have seen a rapid growth in sprawling discount superstores near the interchanges of major highways.

On the one hand, it is clear that these superstores are delivering something many Americans want: good products at low prices. Indeed, these operations could not succeed otherwise. People want and need the jobs they provide. Local governments want the property taxes and sales tax revenues they generate. To the extent that the discount superstores deliver affordable prices, create jobs, and strengthen local tax bases, the National Trust applauds them. They are filling a major market demand and doing so very well indeed.

On the other hand, it is clear that the low prices offered by many superstores include hidden costs. Having worked with local communities across the country on downtown revitalization efforts, the Trust has come to recognize that the scale, location, and design of these stores create major problems. These include:

• sapping the economic vitality of downtowns and main streets by shifting the retail center of gravity out to highway interchanges on the edge of town;

• displacing existing businesses, especially independently owned small businesses that contribute significantly to local civic life, by building stores vastly out of scale with a town's ability to absorb them;

• setting the stage for higher property and state income taxes by creating developments that are costly to serve and require new roads, water and sewer lines, police protection and other public services;

• causing the waste or abandonment of previous public and private investments in existing buildings, streets, parks and other community assets; and

• homogenizing America by building stores that have no relation to their surroundings.

The National Trust recognizes that the retailing world is changing. There are national and global economic forces at work that we cannot control, even if we tried. The Trust recognizes how important low prices and convenient stores are to American consumers, especially to those with modest incomes. In publishing this guide, we seek neither to turn the clock back on retailing nor to deny the advantages of modern retail discounters.

But can the consumer benefits provided by the superstores be achieved only through the creation of more urban sprawl and all that sprawl brings: traffic congestion, automobile dependence, air pollution, dispirited or dead downtowns, despoiled countrysides,

and weakened community ties? Or could some of the benefits be provided without so much damage to the environment and local communities? We think these are questions that should be asked.

The National Trust's goal in publishing this guide is to point out that corporate retailers and communities have choices. National discount retailers can continue to create sprawl, or they can create stores that reinforce existing cities and towns. They can build cookie-cutter buildings that disregard their surroundings, or they can build stores that harmonize with their neighbors. Better yet, they can recycle existing buildings.

Retailers can continue saying to communities: "Here's the national (or regional) formula we use for our stores. Take it or leave it." Or they can listen to citizens and accommodate their desire to preserve the beauty and cohesiveness of their home towns. Retailers can continue to do things a certain way simply because that's how their competitors operate, or they can lead. An example of corporate leadership in the fast-food industry is the decision McDonald's made several years ago to abandon

Communities have choices.

the use of styrofoam containers for meals sold to the public. McDonald's decision made it easier for its competitors to follow suit. There is room for similar leadership in the discount retail industry.

And communities have choices. They can encourage or discourage certain types of development. If a community doesn't want superstore sprawl, it can take steps to prevent it. If a community wants a superstore, it faces a whole host of other questions relating to whether the store comes in on the community's terms. Where should the store be located? How big should it be? How much new retail space can the local economy absorb without suffering the negative fiscal and economic impacts created by a commercial glut? Can the store be designed to help preserve the community's livability and attractiveness? How can the store minimize negative environmental, cultural, scenic, fiscal and economic effects? Above all, what is the long-term impact of the decision?

As this guide makes clear, superstore sprawl is not the only option available to communities that want new growth, development, jobs and tax revenues. Some communities have accepted superstores but required them to fit in with their surroundings. Others have persuaded superstores to re-use historic buildings or to contribute to downtown revitalization programs. Still others have successfully opposed sprawl-type projects and won. The information in this guide is provided for those who would learn from the successes, and the setbacks, of others.

We hope this guide will encourage communities to be more aggressive in protecting the things that make them special, to be more insistent about obtaining the information they need to evaluate superstore proposals. Most of all, we hope to let citizens everywhere know that sprawl is not inevitable and that people can take actions to prevent it.

Richard Moe, President

National Trust for Historic Preservation

May 1994

iii

Below, superstore sprawl in suburban Dayton, Ohio. (Photo: Caleb A. Faux and Pflum, Klausmeier & Gehrum, Cincinnati)

At right, the Church Street Marketplace in downtown Burlington, Vermont. The city opposes superstore sprawl on its outskirts. (Photo: Church Street Marketplace)

Introduction

Every year the National Trust for Historic Preservation publishes a list of "America's 11 Most Endangered Historic Places." One purpose of the list is to draw public attention to important sites facing demolition or some other threat. The more important objective is to get people thinking about why these places are at risk. What public policies or private development practices lie behind the threats? Should these be reexamined? Changed, perhaps?

In June 1993 the Trust put the entire state of Vermont on the "endangered list" because superstore and mall sprawl threatened to destroy characteristics that define Vermont: historic town centers, a well-preserved countryside, working farms, scenic roads, locally owned small businesses, and most importantly, a strong sense of community fostered by compact, cohesive small towns.

Proposals for large, sprawling commercial developments will, if allowed, affect downtowns, main streets, historic districts, small businesses, and farmland throughout Vermont. In addition to the direct effects created by each of the pending developments, there will be broader, longer-term impacts resulting from the legal precedents established by Vermont's handling of these proposals. If the state permits development that radically violates its land-use planning principles, it will be harder to say "no" to similar developments proposed in the future.

Vermont is one of the few American states not already overrun by sprawl. This is no accident. Vermont's citizenry has worked hard to protect the state's distinctive character and its legislature has enacted strong land-use planning laws. Among the principles set forth in Vermont law to guide new development are:

• maintaining the historic settlement pattern of compact villages and urban centers separated by rural countryside,

• discouraging strip development along highways, and

• encouraging energy conservation.

As this is written, superstores and regional malls proposed for Vermont violate every one of these principles. For example, the 156,000-square-foot store planned for St. Albans, Vermont, a historic community of 10,800 people, would not maintain

The historic Denver Dry Goods Building, renovated by Rose Associates of New York, represents an alternative to sprawl. This building provides discount retail, housing and office space. People can get around by foot and public transit because of the downtown location. (Photo: Hooman Aryan)

vi

the compact town center; it would be placed two miles away on rezoned farmland. It would require 44 acres of land for buildings and surface parking, or an area approximately equal to St. Albans' entire downtown. It would generate up to 9,332 automobile trips a day. It would spawn new strip development. It would generate up to 10 tons of solid waste per month, 30 percent of which would not be recycled.[1]

Five such superstores are reportedly planned for Vermont by one national discounter alone.[2] Another six have already been built or are slated for construction just across the state border, close enough to affect Vermont communities for 30 miles around. In addition, developers have proposed to build two regional shopping malls exceeding 400,000 square feet on the outskirts of Rutland and Burlington. All this for a state whose entire population is under 570,000.

The Trust's second purpose in designating Vermont as endangered was to make the American public aware that a long-standing national problem, urban sprawl, has entered a new and more destructive phase with the rapid proliferation of huge discount

stores and retail outlet malls on the edges of traditional cities and towns. The designation was, in effect, a wake-up call intended to ask Americans if they really want a new generation of automobile-oriented sprawl—"super-sprawl," this time—or whether they'd like to encourage a more benign type of development.

Some people might ask: Isn't it rather late to be sounding this alarm? Hasn't most of America already been overtaken by sprawl? To be sure, sprawl has indeed devastated many communities already, as empty downtown buildings and degraded countrysides across the country attest. But many communities remain relatively intact. For these places, it is still possible to adopt the physician's maxim and "do no harm." Moreover, even communities already surrounded by sprawl will have opportunities in the future to undo previous damage. As old strip shopping centers and old malls require new facelifts or other renovations, their undesirable features can be corrected. There are many ways to repair the damage sprawl has already done to our communities.

The public response to the Trust's designation of Vermont indicated

that people all over America are concerned about sprawl. In a *Spokesman Review* column headlined, "Coeur d'Alene On Way to Becoming 'Sprawl-Mart'," Chris Peck from Spokane, Washington wrote:

Maybe it hasn't been declared [endangered] yet, but I think Coeur d'Alene's unique scenic and historic character is now threatened. The lakes, the trees, the dirt roads are what make the panhandle unlike anything else. Yet I feel this very sense of place is now on the verge of being lost.[3]

Citizens from places like Seattle, Washington; Sandpoint, Idaho; Lebanon, New Hampshire; Hyde Park, New York; Sandwich, Massachusetts; Kingsport, Tennessee; Marshall, Texas; Eagle River, Alaska; and Danville, Kentucky, called the Trust to say their communities, too, were threatened by superstore sprawl, and could the Trust help them?

While citizens in all regions of the country are clearly concerned about the homogenizing effects of superstore sprawl, many question what, if anything, they can do about it. When they speak out against sprawl, they are often told that it is "inevitable," or that their opposition is tantamount to opposing jobs and a healthy tax base because it impedes new growth and development.

Sprawl is not synonymous with growth and development, and not all development produces a net increase in jobs or tax revenues. New development that is appropriately sized for the community in which it locates, that makes good use of existing buildings and infrastructures, that minimizes harm to the natural environment, and that fits in sensitively with its neighbors, makes good economic sense. The National Trust favors such development and, in fact, believes it is desperately needed in many cities and towns. Development that exceeds a community's capacity to absorb it, that triggers the abandonment of prior public and private investments, helps neither the local economy nor the local tax base in the long run. Meanwhile, it debases resources that might brace future economic development initiatives. It's called killing the goose that lays the golden eggs.

Large commercial developments that are radically out of scale with a community's existing stores can disrupt the local economy and change a town's way of life. Given that local residents will have to live with the consequences of such disruption for many years, it is reasonable for them to insist that their elected officials address questions regarding the long-term effects of this type of development.

As National Trust President Richard Moe has pointed out, communities have choices. They can steer new growth into areas where it is needed and away from areas where it will do harm. They can welcome new development but insist that developers refrain from destroying historic and scenic resources that citizens value. Communities have planning, zoning, negotiation and other tools at their disposal for preserving (or creating) humane environments for people to live in. And they have a responsibility to use them.

Cities and towns across America contain old and historic mills, warehouses, railroad stations and other large structures that could house major discount stores. In many cases, it would not only be appropriate for national discount retailers to rehabilitate and reuse these older buildings, but it would also help to revive languishing urban centers. Although recycling old buildings for modern

It is within our power to stop the blight of ever more sprawl on the American landscape.

retail uses does require more creativity than putting up a one-level box in the middle of a cornfield, some developers and retailers have demonstrated a willingness to be creative and to consider the long-term interests and desires of the community in which they locate. T.J. Maxx recently moved into a historic building in downtown Denver. Home Depot is preserving the art deco facade of a historic market building in downtown Tulsa. Lechmere, a New England-based discount chain, has built a three-level structure that fits in well with an urban neighborhood in Cambridge, Mass. Projects such as these are encouraging examples of corporate efforts to preserve community landmarks and be better neighbors.

This guide discusses economic, social, and environmental reasons for reducing or preventing superstore sprawl. It describes zoning, planning, and other tools citizens can use to stop or abate sprawl. It offers guidance on how to deal with the media—a critical element to any local sprawl-containment effort. It includes case studies to illustrate how individual communities opposed sprawl and revived their downtowns. And it lists organizations and publications that may serve as useful resources to local citizens.

The guide's overriding message, however, is that *it is within our power* to stop the blight of ever more sprawl on the American landscape and to breathe new life into older cities and towns. Our cities and towns hold the key to what the environmentalists call "sustainable development"— really, just a way of creating new jobs and businesses so that future generations will be able to support themselves and enjoy this country's beauty.

ix

By making it difficult or dangerous for people to walk, public policies can contribute to sprawl and auto dependence. Although the city of Asheville, N.C., asked for a sidewalk alongside this road when it was being widened, state transportation policy will not permit construction of sidewalks if they were not already present unless the city pays for them. Thus this lady and her dog must walk in the roadway. (Photo: Julian Price, CityWatch)

Part One

Implications of Superstore Sprawl

Chapter One

Sprawl and Superstores: An Overview

Every community wants a stronger economy. With more money, a community can provide better schools, better services, and a better overall quality of life for its citizens. We expect new development—new jobs, new businesses, new industries—to help provide those economic benefits for our communities. But development comes in many forms, and each form has its own set of costs. The challenge involves encouraging new development to take place in ways that build on a community's existing resources rather than duplicating or destroying them. Opposing sprawl does not mean opposing economic development. In fact, it means exactly the opposite. It means guiding development in a manner that maximizes the economic benefits to a community.

What is Sprawl?

This guide defines sprawl as low-density, land-consumptive, automobile-oriented development located on the outskirts of cities and towns. Sprawl is a product of both public policies and private development practices. This guide focuses on the latter, but a few words on policy-caused sprawl are in order.

Causes of Sprawl: Public Policies and Private Development Practices

Federal policies. Over the past 50 years, the Federal Government has put in place a broad range of programs that have had the effect, whether intended or not, of fostering costly and wasteful land-use practices. The Federal Government promotes sprawl through its housing policies, water and sewer grants, office location decisions, but mostly through its transportation policies.

For decades Washington encouraged America's auto dependence by promoting and subsidizing highway construction while failing to prevent the deterioration of rail transportation, public transit, and inter-city bus service. Although the Intermodal Surface Transportation Efficiency Act (ISTEA) passed by Congress in 1991 moves away from the statutory bias favoring highways over all other modes of transportation, highways still receive the lion's share of federal money. ISTEA requires state and local governments to consider the impact of transportation on land use, but not the impact of land use and urban design policies on transportation. Yet these policies are the horse, not the cart. They either open up or foreclose opportunities for reducing automobile dependence and the sprawl that it creates.

Road design standards written by the American Association of State Highway and Transportation Officials and applied by most states promote sprawl by effectively mandating that streets be wider and more land-consumptive than necessary. These standards, which gloss over the safety of pedestrians, have undercut efforts to make communities more walkable.

The General Services Administration contributes to sprawl when it relocates federal agencies from older downtowns to the outer suburbs.[4] So does the U. S. Postal Service when it unnecessarily abandons downtown and village center post offices for new buildings out by the interstates.

State policies. State transportation agencies contribute to sprawl by adhering to policies that unreasonably favor vehicular over pedestrian and public transportation modes. Communities are frequently pressed to accept road widenings that destroy compact, walkable main streets and encourage commercial strip development in outlying areas.[5] Often when local governments turn to the state

for help in repairing existing roads, they are told, "Yes, the state will help pay for the repairs, but only if you accept our plan to widen your main street, narrow your sidewalks, bulldoze your street trees, and eliminate the on-street parking that customers use to patronize your local stores." This all-too-common scenario destroys the cohesiveness, pedestrian friendliness, and economic vitality of downtown main streets.

Also, like the federal General Services Administration, states are moving offices out of downtowns and into the suburbs, where they are accessible only by automobile. These actions weaken the economic health of the urban core, abet the push of new development into the countryside, and leave empty buildings behind.

Local policies. Local governments contribute to sprawl in various ways as well. Decisions by county governments to locate new courthouses on the outskirts of town help to foster sprawl. So do decisions by local school boards to locate and design schools so they are reachable only by car or school bus.

Well-crafted zoning policies are essential tools for protecting a

It is against the law in much of America to build tightly-knit communities that people love—places they feature on Christmas cards, places they visit by the millions in Europe, such as Salzburg and Paris, places like Cape Cod, Beacon Hill, downtown San Francisco and Charleston (S.C.).

Indices of Sprawl and Commercial Glut

Nationwide, three million acres of farmland are converted to other use every year. (Source: Timothy Egan, "Farmers Resist Paving their Fertile Valley," The New York Times, December 4, 1989.)

• The nation currently has the equivalent of 3,800 vacant shopping centers. (Source: Land Use Digest, Vol. 25, No. 11, November 1992. Urban Land Institute)

• Between 1950 and 1980, when the American population increased by 50 percent, the number of their automobiles increased by 200 percent. (Source: Kenneth T. Jackson, The Crabgrass Frontier. Oxford University Press, 1985.)

• More than one-third of the Los Angeles area is consumed by highways, parking lots, and interchanges; in the downtown section this proportion rises to two-thirds. (Source: Jackson, ibid.)

• Nationally, from 1958 to 1989, the Federal Government spent $213 billion on highways, but only $23 billion on railroads and mass transit. (Source: Scott Bernstein, "Imagining Equity: Using ISTEA and the Clean Air Act,"

Environment and Development, American Planning Association, December 1993)

• From 1970 to 1990, the amount of land consumed for development in the Chicago area increased by 55 percent while the population rose by only 4 percent. Northeastern Illinois lost 444 square miles, or nearly one-fourth of its farmland, during this period. (Source: Bernstein, ibid.)

• By 1990, shopping center vacancies were running at almost 12 percent nationwide. Nevertheless, nearly 300 million square feet more was added that year to the nation's shopping center inventory, which comes out to a rate of a major 34,000-square-foot store every hour. At nearly 4.6 billion square feet of total store space, there is about 20 square feet for every person in America. A good half-billion of it sits empty. (Source: Robert Goodman, "The Dead Mall," Metropolis, November 1993)

• The shopping center industry is faced with excessive capacity. In response to the conspicuous consumption of the 1980s, retail floor space in North America grew

by 80 percent, supported by only a 10 percent increase in population. (Source: Ian F. Thomas, "Reinventing the Regional Mall," Urban Land, February 1994)

• Houston provides nearly 30 parking spaces per city resident while Detroit provides 13. Paris and Amsterdam, by comparison, provide only one space for every three central city residents. (Source: Peter W. G. Newman and Jeffrey R. Kenworthy, Cities and Automobile Dependence: An International Sourcebook [Brookfield, Vermont: Gower Press, 1989]. See Marcia D. Lowe, "Reclaiming Cities for People," World Watch, July/August 1992.)

• Every car needs an estimated 4,000 square feet of asphalt for parking and turning at home, work, and shopping. (Source: The End of the Road, by David G. Burwell et al. National Wildlife Federation. 1977)

3

community's distinctive character, but those that make it impractical to move about except by car may work against this objective.[6] By requiring inappropriately large front, side and rear yard setbacks, zoning ordinances often create excessive distances between buildings. Zoning ordinances that rigidly segregate residential areas from shops and stores, no matter how well-designed, virtually guarantee a community's auto-dependence. By allowing leap-frog development, zoning ordinances make it economically impossible for municipalities to provide public transit. That's because transit can succeed only where development is sufficiently dense and compact. By requiring parking spaces whose land area exceeds the entire square footage of the buildings they serve, zoning ordinances contribute still further to sprawl.

It is against the law in much of America to build tightly-knit communities that people love—places they feature on Christmas cards, places they visit by the millions in Europe, such as Salzburg and Paris, places like Cape Cod, Beacon Hill, downtown San Francisco and Charleston (S.C.).

Private Development Practices

Superstores and Value Retailing While recognizing that public policies figure prominently in the creation of sprawl, this guide focuses on private development practices. Its specific focus is the "superstore sprawl" being promoted so aggressively today by large national discount stores known variously as "value retailers," "superstores," "big box retailers" and "category killers."

Most of these stores have certain characteristics in common. First, they are very big. They range in size from 90,000 to 200,000 square feet or more. They generally do not locate downtown, but when they do, they sometimes simply bring sprawl into the city and overwhelm existing stores and buildings. They prefer to locate on land (often rezoned farmland) near the exits of interstate highways, even when vacant commercial space exists downtown. They generally use the same store design (typically, a windowless box) everywhere, regardless of its incompatibility with the surroundings. They usually insist on a single-floor layout, so the stores spread out over several acres. Neither located nor designed so people can walk or ride a bus to them, they require vast expanses of surface parking.

In *Urban Land* magazine, development analyst Dean Schwanke describes these discount superstores as "big-box 'power retailers' with strong advertising and promotional programs, and . . . oriented toward high volume rather than [price] markup as the way to make money."[7] He classifies them according to three subgroups:

Discount Department Stores: These discounters sell department store merchandise at low prices. Examples include Wal-Mart, Kmart, and Target.

Category Killers: These are large specialty retailers that buy and sell in huge volumes at low prices. Many of them have direct relationships with product manufacturers so they can eliminate middleman charges. Examples include Toys R Us, Circuit City, Crown Books, Home Depot, Sports Authority and Builders Square.

Warehouse Clubs. These are membership clubs that offer a variety of goods—groceries, electronics, office supplies, clothing, hardware and jewelry—at wholesale prices. Unlike discount department stores, which sell as many as 60,000 items, warehouse clubs provide a more limited menu of 3,000 to 5,000 items. Three warehouse clubs dominate this industry: Sam's Club, Price-Costco and Pace. These stores range in size from 104,000 to 170,000 square feet and serve markets of up to 250,000 people.

People often refer to all three of these subgroups of discount stores as "superstores" because they are so big. This is the term this guide will use for huge discount stores — whether they be discount department stores, "category killers" or membership clubs.

"Power centers" are the large (250,000 to 750,000 square foot) centers in which superstores sometimes congregate.

Studies have shown that superstore profits often come at the expense of existing merchants, especially small businesses. The figures below are drawn from research into the experience of Iowa towns with a super-discounter selling general merchandise. Money generated by local stores typically recirculates in the community; that generated by superstores often goes directly to out-of-town corporate headquarters. (Source of figures: Kenneth E. Stone, Professor of Economics, Iowa State University)

$20M

Annual sales of discount general merchandise store

(Estimated average)

$9M

Increase in annual sales of town as a whole

(Actual average)

$11M

Loss in sales by existing merchants

(Estimated average)

Chapter Two

Problems with Superstores and Sprawl

Even after a customer drives to a superstore project, the development's design and layout discourage walking from one store to another. The distances are short enough to walk, but there are few, if any, pedestrian amenities.

To many people, the new trend in what the development industry calls "value retailing" is an unmixed blessing. The big discounters create new jobs. They generate tax revenues for local governments. They offer a wide selection of high-quality merchandise at low prices. They're efficient. They're accessible. They're convenient. Who could quarrel with all this?

No one. Virtually everybody, preservationists included, wants jobs, healthy tax bases, growing economies and good bargains on good products. These benefits are not the problem.

The problem is that in providing these benefits, superstores can also do a lot of damage. This damage falls into five major categories: economic, fiscal, environmental, social and cultural.

Economic and Fiscal Impacts

The economic damage caused by superstore sprawl stems from a fairly simple economic principle: If more commercial space is built in a community than the local economy can absorb, a glut occurs and the new space simply displaces existing businesses and jobs. As Jane Jacobs, author of the urban planning classic, *The Death and Life of Great American Cities*, has pointed out:

a sudden major increase of commercial space will inevitably lead to vacancies in existing buildings and probably also to failures among existing shops. . . Only a city growing very rapidly can absorb a new downtown mall which is not at the expense of its existing downtown. . . In effect the mall must rob Peter to pay Paul.[8]

Kenneth E. Stone, an economist at Iowa State University, studied the effects of super "discount general merchandise" stores on small towns in Iowa. Estimating that such a store averaged annual sales of $20 million,[9] he found that the host town's total sales rose by only $9 million. His conclusion: existing merchants lost $11 million. (See chart, opposite page.) Stone also found that within five years of a superstore's opening, small towns within 20 miles suffered a net loss in sales of 19.2 percent. Small towns farther away, but still within the superstore's market, experienced losses of 10.1 percent.[10]

A 1989 study of superstores in Colorado found that most communities hosting a new superstore experienced overall increases in retail sales, but these gains occurred at the expense of existing businesses. Discount department stores on the fringes of small towns exert the same impacts that regional shopping centers had on larger cities years ago, according to this study.[11] Those impacts were devastating. In Hagerstown, Maryland, for example, downtown retail sales declined by 31 percent following the opening of a 570,000-square-foot mall in 1974.[12] In Plattsburgh, New York, not only did downtown retail sales fall dramatically after a new mall opened, but so did downtown commercial property values: by 32 percent (or 60 percent in real terms) between 1970 and 1978. Plattsburgh's downtown has still not recovered.[13]

In a nutshell, the construction of too much retail space does not enlarge the economic pie. Often it simply reallocates the pie, with superstores taking mega-bites and local small businesses eating the crumbs.

But don't the new superstores simply represent a form of economic Darwinism? Aren't they successful because they are smarter, more efficient, better retailers? In some ways, yes, and to that extent they deserve credit. But as Donella H. Meadows, an adjunct professor at Dartmouth, points out:

There are two ways to cut costs. You can reduce waste and inefficiency. That's great. It's what makes the market system go round. But you can also cut costs by putting them off onto someone or something else. You can build cheap, ugly buildings that no one wants to live near or look at. You can muscle down your suppliers' prices, so they have to move production to poor communities and pay wages that won't support a decent life. You can hire part-time workers with no benefits and give them no training. Our taxes or insurance fees will pay for their health care[14] ... You can pressure towns for tax breaks and free roads and water lines and sewers. The other taxpayers will pick up the bill. You can pay only a fraction of the real costs of materials and energy. Nature will eat the damage.

This kind of cost-cutting not only imposes injustices on others, it also undermines the market economy. It distorts prices so consumers cannot make rational decisions. It rewards bigness and power, rather than real efficiency.[15]

Often overlooked is the fact that

Spontaneous play is becoming a thing of the past in many areas of the country due to sprawl. Children have to be driven miles to play with friends.

8

money generated by locally owned stores gets recycled within the community. The money raised by out-of-state superstores but quickly whisked away to corporate headquarters is money that doesn't recirculate through the local economy.

Small businesses in America are struggling today. One major reason is competition from superstores. Small, independently owned retailers often have very slim profit margins. A superstore that drains off as little as 10 to 15 percent of such a business's gross sales can put the business out of business.

Many people see the proliferation of superstores and "value retailers" as "The American Way" and economic progress. But is the homogenization of the economy really the American way? What happens to low discount prices after thousands of small businesses are killed off and only a few national companies remain in existence?

To be sure, many individual entrepreneurs are inefficient and deserve to be replaced by more efficient operations. Nonetheless, small business *as a type* of free enterprise has been an important part of the American

culture. It has also contributed to economic diversity, an important community asset when a large employer closes its doors.

While not favoring one individual business over another, communities can enact public policies that enable local entrepreneurs to launch, build up and sustain small businesses. Public policies can also aim to retain a measure of economic diversity in the local economy.[16]

Finally, it's worth pointing out that local business owners who live in a community have an allegiance to, and stake in it. They serve on local boards, run for city council, and provide leadership for the community. Superstore managers are often relocated in just a few years. Their allegiance is to their career. Their advancement to a higher position in another store depends on their profitable management of the chain store, not on furthering the well-being of the community.[17]

Environment and Energy Impacts

Like other forms of sprawl, superstore sprawl harms the environment and depletes energy supplies because of one simple fact: people can seldom get

to superstores except by driving. Driving requires gas and oil. It requires new roads, wider roads. (See sidebar, p. 13.)

Superstores usually stand apart from a city or town center. They are designed to be inaccessible to pedestrians, and they are too remote from the homes of their shoppers to be within walking distance. Cost-effective public transit is not an option because the market served by such stores is too widely dispersed and spread out.

Even after a customer drives to a superstore project, the development's design and layout discourage walking from one store to another. The distances are short enough to walk, but there are few, if any, pedestrian amenities such as sidewalks, crosswalks, and favorable traffic signals. Curb cuts with cars darting in and out make pedestrians feel like hounded rabbits. With trees leveled from the site, minimal landscaping, huge parking lots, and long blank walls with nothing interesting for people to look at, walking is not only dangerous but also tedious. Often four, six, or even eight lanes of busy traffic separate stores, so that walking from a Kmart to a Burger King across the

9

highway is unpleasant at best and hazardous at worst. It is not uncommon for people to hop into a car to drive as little as 1/8 of a mile.[18]

A 110,000-square-foot shopping center can generate as many as 946 car trips per hour and 9,710 trips per day.[19]

Few Americans would argue in favor of eliminating the use of the car for shopping, and that is certainly not the argument being made here. Many steps can be taken, however, to reduce automobile usage and to *avoid increasing* automobile dependence in the future.

Social and Cultural Impacts

The discarding of walkable or "transit-serveable" downtowns in favor of drive-to commercial strips causes social and cultural problems as well.

There are many Americans who lack auto mobility, or who for social or safety reasons should not feel compelled to drive. When communities are arranged with no other options for getting around, these people can have a hard time.

Consider the elderly. Due to failing eyesight and hearing problems, many elderly people cannot drive or are afraid to do so. Being unable to drive means social isolation and loss of independence, conditions that geron-tologists have long associated with premature institutionalization of the elderly.

Consider children. Spontaneous play is becoming a thing of the past in many areas of the country due to sprawl. As a *Washington Post* article observes:

Suburban developments are so sprawling that in many places neigh-borhood games are all but obsolete. Children have to be driven miles to play with friends, requiring intricate planning and plenty of time.[20]

Consider the poor. Transportation (mostly auto-related expenses) cost the average American household $5,228, or over $400 a month, in 1992.[21] This exceeded the cost of food and ranked next to the biggest household expense: housing. For many people, the burden of paying for, maintaining and driving a car[22] not only negates some of the financial savings said to be provided by "value retailers," but it also adds to their mental stress. Health care agencies have begun to add traffic congestion to their checklists of stress sources for clients to fill out when they sign up for counseling.[23]

The traffic generated by a superstore affects far more than the immediately surrounding area. It generates pressures to widen and straighten roads throughout an entire region. The new roads, road widenings, and parking lots needed to serve this traffic may necessitate the loss of homes and historic buildings or the impairment of their settings. They may also destroy trees and other valued features of the landscape.

Problems Resulting from Size & Location of Superstores

Superstores that establish new commercial centers do more than change traffic patterns. They change social patterns, too. A newspaper account of a Keene, N.H., grocery store's decision to move away from the town center to an outlying shopping center quotes a local restau-rant owner on the social conse-quences to the town of this decision:

The IGA [grocery store] completed a social circle and that aspect has been removed. It was a common place for people in town to see each other. It brought the town together. You could count on seeing the same people at certain times of the day.... [The focus of the new IGA on the outskirts of town] is now multi-town. When I go to the IGA I see different faces all the time. It used to be I would know everyone in there and say hello to them.[24]

Another Keene resident comments:

The people who work for the [new] store don't know you anymore. It's, 'Excuse me, sir, what's your number?' It used to be, 'Hey, Bill, how's it going?' " [25]

Writing in Urban Land,[26] urban designer Alex Achimore expresses the problem this way:

Since the 1930s, low prices and automobile accessibility have been emphasized over service and amenities not vital to retail sales. And strip retail, by offering lower prices than possible in Main Street's mom-and-pop stores, has arguably contributed to postwar gains in (material) living standards.

But other important aspects of daily life were lost along the way to retail efficiency. Paramount among these is the loss of "habitat" for community functions. In older town centers, retail

was the glue that connected a myriad of public places—government offices, parks, schools, libraries, and so forth. The intermingling of retail and community facilities created a setting for repetitive chance encounters with friends and neighbors that built and strengthened community bonds. Single-purpose retail establishments may be great for retailing, but the absence from them of reasons for lingering and places in which to linger has contributed to the atrophy of community and neighborhood activities.

William H. Whyte, one of the nation's keenest observers of cities and human behavior, emphasizes the value of central gathering places in his book *City: Rediscovering the Center.* There he writes:

...as the city has been losing functions it has been reasserting its most ancient one: a place where people come together, face-to-face.

More than ever, the center is the place for news and gossip, for the creation of ideas...for hatching deals, for starting parades. This is the stuff of the public life of the city..

[T]his human congress is the genius of the place, its reason for being, its great

> **"But other important aspects of daily life were lost along the way to retail efficiency. Paramount among these is the loss of "habitat" for community functions."**
> **—Alex Achimore**

11

marginal edge. This is the engine, the city's true export. Whatever makes this congress easier, more spontaneous, more enjoyable is not at all a frill. It is the heart of the center of the city.[27]

The size of superstores not only has economic consequences for existing small businesses, as noted earlier, but social consequences, too. Kenneth Munsell, director of the Small Towns Institute in Ellensburg, Washington, makes these observations:

There is no way to deny that some of the superstores do a better job than some local businesses. But they do it in a very destructive manner. Penney's and Sears did not destroy the towns they entered in an earlier era. They added options. They complemented what was already there. Their scale was not so huge that they precluded the sale by others of virtually all other merchandise. The superstores are destroying a large segment of the middle class. They are turning independent shop owners into $5 an hour clerks. What we are seeing is downtowns, normally the center of a community, now catering increasingly to tourists. The smaller stores sell trinkets. They have specialty shops. But they are no longer relevant to the needs of the community. And this is

the best scenario. That's wrong. It shows no real understanding of what downtown is. It's far more significant than just a retail center.

Newspaper and magazine articles on superstores are replete with stories about the loss of local leadership and charitable contributions to community causes that follows when a local economy becomes glutted and independent businesses go broke. As columnist Jim Cory observes in *Hardware Age:*

[W]hen downtown businesses fold [as a result of superstores] there goes the newspaper's advertising base. And not only that. There go the businesses that help pay for the Little League's new uniforms and the Scout troop's new tents, that help support all the activities that make up the life of a community.[28]

Communities need focal points, or central gathering places, to facilitate the repeated face-to-face encounters people need to get to know one another. Towns with places where people can "meet and greet" encourage such encounters. Settlements that scatter people hither and yon stunt the development of a sense of community.

12

"Penney's and Sears did not destroy the towns they entered in an earlier era. They added options. They complemented what was already there. Their scale was not so huge that they precluded the sale by others of virtually all other merchandise."

—Kenneth Munsell

Costs of Auto Dependence:
A Cause and Effect of Sprawl[29]

- Automobiles cause between 40 and 60 percent of all urban smog and 80 percent of all carbon monoxide emissions.

- One hundred million Americans live in urban areas with unhealthy levels of smog.

- Air conditioning for automobiles generated 120 million pounds of ozone-depleting chlorofluorocarbons in 1986.

- 138,000 tons of lead from used automobile batteries were discarded in 1988.

- 80 million gallons of oil were spilled in U.S. waters between 1980 and 1986. The typical recovery rate for spilled oil is less than 15 percent.

- 200 to 250 million tires are discarded annually, while 250 billion tires have already accumulated in existing tire piles.[30]

- Every time a person fills up and uses a tank of gas in a medium-sized American car, he deposits in the atmosphere the equivalent of a 100-pound sack of pure carbon, 5.6 pounds for every gallon of gasoline.[31]

- Cars and other vehicles powered by fossil fuels generated 492.0 million metric tons of carbon dioxide, one of the greenhouse gases linked to global warming, in 1990.[32]

- Motor vehicle crashes cost the nation $137 billion, or over 2 percent of the gross domestic product, in 1990. Of this, $13.9 billion went for medical bills.[33]

- Motor vehicle crashes occur once every 19 seconds in the U.S. In 1993, 39,850 Americans died in motor vehicle accidents. Millions more were injured and disabled.[34]

Cars dominate the landscape outside Indianapolis. (Photo: Caleb Faux)

14

When a sprawling store closes its doors—
often due to the commerical glut
resulting from overbuilding—this is what
a community can be left with.

Chapter Three

The Modus Operandi of Supersprawl Promoters

A rezoning request might simply refer to "retail and light industry," leaving the average citizen without a clue as to the true nature of a project in the works.

Interviews with local planners, citizen activists, mayors, small business people and others reveal a pattern of aggressive tactics used by promoters of superstore sprawl. Described below is a scenario commonly recounted by citizens with first-hand experience in dealing with superstores. Some of the practices noted here are not unique to promoters of superstore sprawl; they apply to many types of real estate development. While these practices may be perfectly legal, they illustrate the difficulties citizens often encounter in trying to moderate the negative impacts of superstore sprawl.

A Common Scenario

The national discount chain contacts a commercial real estate broker and developer in a target market area. The broker makes discreet inquiries among local landowners (often farmers) to ascertain their interest in selling a land option to a developer.

The identity of the discounter may not be publicized lest its disclosure inflate the price of the land. The negative impacts of the development are often downplayed and are not well-known or understood by citizens.

With a land option in hand, the discounter's developer-partner asks the local government to rezone agricultural (or industrial or residential) land to commercial uses. A rezoning request might simply refer to "retail and light industry," leaving the average citizen without a clue as to the true nature of the project in the works. The local governing body may approve the rezoning—or a water and sewer line extension to serve the new development—without even knowing whether a superstore is involved.[35]

After the rezoning is approved—or if it is unnecessary—the developer files a site plan with the local planning department. This plan discloses many details about the project. It gives the size, configuration and layout of the proposed superstore. It reveals the number and location of parking spaces, the number and height of light poles, the landscaping plan, the plan for handling crankcase oil run-off from the parking lot, and the building design. It also says how much traffic the developer expects the project to generate and explains the plan for mitigating traffic impacts.

Sometimes citizens get wind of what's happening during public hearings typically required for rezonings. Often they don't learn about the superstore until after the site plan review process begins. Sometimes they don't know about the project until they drive past the site one day and see bulldozers clearing it of trees.

By this time, however, the developer may already have had many discussions with the local planning department and city (or county or town) council officials, during which he has touted the project's economic benefits. With information often provided by the national chain, the developer predicts the store will create many new jobs and thousands of dollars in property tax and sales revenues. The developer may offer to pay for new roads to handle traffic generated in the superstore's immediate area (but not beyond it). He might even throw in a small grant to the downtown merchants association, which by now is scared stiff of the potentially negative impacts of the superstore on downtown. To many officials grappling with tight budgets, these benefits seem irresistible.

When citizens speak out against the proposed project, they are often accused of being elitist, anti-job, anti-development, anti-property rights, anti-progress, or all of the above. They may encounter hostility from the local newspaper. This hostility may stem from the paper's genuine belief that the project will benefit the community, or it may spring from the hope that the superstore will generate new advertising revenues.

Downtown merchants likely to be hurt by the creation of superstore sprawl are often reluctant to speak out. They fear alienating customers. They feel their opposition will seem self-serving or "anti-free enterprise." Or they feel intimidated by powerful development and financial interests in the community. If a citizens' group shows real promise of persuading the city (or county or town) council to reject the project, the developer may encourage candidates who support it to run for public office. Some communities have reported that national companies have hired public relations firms to influence the outcome of local policy decisions on superstores.[36]

During the site plan review process, citizens may ask the planning commission to have the developer make changes to the project. For

18

Downtown merchants likely to be hurt by the creation of superstore sprawl are often reluctant to speak out. They fear alienating customers. They feel their opposition will seem self-serving or "anti-free enterprise." Or they may feel intimidated by powerful development and financial interests in the community.

example, they might ask that the size of the building—or the number of parking spaces—be reduced in order to preserve a stand of trees. Or they might ask that the design of the building harmonize better with its surroundings. The developer may respond by agreeing to paint the cinderblock structure in earth tones instead of primary colors. Or he may say he personally would love to make the requested changes, but his tenant (the still unidentified national company) will not go along with them. If his tenant backs out, the community risks losing the promised jobs and tax revenues—benefits by now eagerly awaited. Does the city council really want to risk throwing away these economic benefits, the developer will ask, hinting broadly that if the tenant "walks," it might just go to the neighboring community, in which case the community will get none of the development's promised benefits and many of its burdens: traffic congestion, air pollution, and loss of business.

By now the so-called "property rights" issue may also have surfaced. The landowner who wants to sell out, the developer, the national company and their lawyers may argue that citizens and local officials who oppose the project are interfering with private property rights. They may argue that a property owner should be allowed to use his land exactly as he pleases, ignoring the fact that one owner's actions may affect the rights of others. The developer may even threaten to sue the local government if it refuses to rezone the land. Or he may just subtly hint that such refusal is unconstitutional and represents a "taking" of private property for which the locality might be held liable.[37] Either way, local public officials are intimidated.

By the time the debate is settled, community residents may feel deeply divided. Such division is a major legacy of superstore sprawl and takes time to heal.

Ways to respond to these challenges are discussed in the following chapters.

19

A sprawling regional shopping center in suburban Cincinnati. (Photo: Caleb A. Faux & Pflum, Klausmeier & Gehrum)

Chapter Four

Local, State, and Federal Laws

Part Two: Strategy

As noted at the outset of this guide, your community has choices. It can welcome a superstore on the store's terms, no questions asked. It can welcome the superstore but insist that the store come in on the community's terms. Or it can oppose the construction of superstores altogether. In many cases, you will want to find out what leverage your community has (or doesn't have) to negotiate with the superstore. This involves gathering information about the proposed development and identifying laws your community can use to minimize sprawl or prevent it altogether.

Information Gathering

People first learn about superstore development proposals in different ways: by reading the newspaper, by talking to friends or local officials, or sometimes simply by noticing engineers doing survey work across the street from their homes or in their neighborhood. Regardless of how you hear the news, your first step is to find out everything you possibly can about the pending development proposal. In doing so, it may be useful to form a core group of concerned citizens so that you can share information and chart strategies with each other at the

outset. Has a developer filed a rezoning application or a site plan with the local planning board? If so, get a copy of the relevant documents and read them. If not, talk to your planning commissioners and/or staff members (preferably ones sympathetic to preservation). Ask them to tell you what they know about the project and to describe the planning process it must undergo. Ask whether a rezoning is needed or whether the desired land is already zoned for large-scale commercial purposes. Ask how many public hearings must be held and when they might occur. Find out whether the developer needs any special state or federal reviews relating to environmental, transportation, wetlands, coastal zone, historic preservation or other issues. Must the state approve curb cuts into state highways?

Meanwhile, try to get a sense of how individual members of the planning board staff, planning commission, and local governing body feel about the project. If they must vote on the project, you will want to identify who favors it, who opposes it, and who sits on the fence. Try to learn what specific concerns the fence-sitters have; you may be able to address these concerns and win these people over.

Step Two is to find out what local policies governing new development already exist. These will typically be explained in two documents: a local comprehensive plan and a zoning ordinance. Many local comprehensive plans and zoning ordinances provide useful hooks for combatting sprawl. Others offer citizens little of any use. The best way to find out whether your community's plan and zoning ordinance help or not is to read them. These are public documents, so you should have little difficulty getting copies. You may have to pay a nominal charge.

22

Local Laws

Local Comprehensive Plan. The plan is intended to project an overall vision for the community's growth, development and preservation. It articulates local public policy and lets property owners, businesses, conservationists and other citizens know such things as:

• where new development will be encouraged, discouraged, or even prohibited

• how certain areas will be zoned—i.e.,

commercially, residentially, industrially, or for a mixture of land uses

• what criteria apply to new development proposals

• how dense the development in certain areas may be

• how big buildings can be

• where new roads (or road widenings) are planned

• what historic, scenic, or environmentally sensitive areas should be protected.

The plan often includes discrete sections on various aspects of community development, including land use, housing, economic development, natural resources and transportation. Many plans contain a special section on historic preservation; others integrate preservation policies into other major sections; still others ignore preservation altogether.

You should read the plan from cover to cover and take notes while doing so. Identify statements in the plan that could help or hurt your effort to contain sprawl and preserve

community character. For example, Kent County, Maryland's plan includes among its objectives "support [for] small, locally owned businesses" and "prevent[ion of] commercial sprawl outside the county's existing traditional commercial centers." The plan governing Barnstable, Massachusetts, calls for "compact forms of development" and prohibits "strip commercial development outside of designated growth centers."

Consider whether the plan limits new construction or road building in fragile historic or environmentally sensitive areas. Does it place any overall restrictions on the amount of new development allowed? What, if anything, does it say about the size of new retail development? About the size and location of buildings?[38]

A good plan will contain strong policy statements that citizens can quote to good effect during public hearings on a proposed development. Quoting directly from the plan can serve both political and legal purposes. Although examples abound of local governments spending thousands of dollars on plans and then ignoring them, many public officials do believe in the value of planning and will want

The burden of proof is on the person seeking a rezoning, not on the local city or county council. It is reasonable and entirely legal for the local government to deny a rezoning unless this burden of proof is met.

to adhere to the policies in their local plan, whether they agree with you or not. It may be useful to find out how much the plan cost to develop, when it was adopted, and which officials favored its adoption. Officials particularly involved in the plan may be potential allies.

The plan may provide political and legal protection for public officials being pressured to approve harmful rezonings. It takes them off the hook and enables them to say, "We'd love to approve this rezoning, but our community went through a long and involved process to develop a consensus regarding its future growth, and I think we should stick with our official plan." Some states require that local zoning decisions conform to local comprehensive plans. Such "consistency" requirements sometimes give citizens an important legal hook for opposing inappropriate rezonings.

The plan's legal importance stems from the fact that courts generally require that zoning decisions be reasonable and fair, and that individual property owners not be unfairly singled out to bear burdens not borne by other owners in similar situations. A good plan can help a

community demonstrate what the courts refer to as "reasonableness" and "fairness"—defenses against lawsuits alleging "arbitrary and capricious" zoning decisions. (See Lawrence, Kansas, case study, Chapter 10.[39]) But whether the plan helps or not, you should know what it says and doesn't say.

Zoning ordinance. The zoning ordinance governs where certain types of new development can go and where they can't. Typically, certain areas are designated for commercial, residential, or industrial land uses or for a combination thereof. The ordinance also establishes minimum lot sizes for buildings. It says how far back from, or close to, the street a building must be located. It limits the bulk and height of commercial structures. It requires a specific number of parking spaces for so many square feet of retail space. It indicates what, if any, special conditions new development must meet. It governs the size and location of signs. It may require a developer to preserve mature trees on a development site, or to comply with certain design guidelines for new construction. It may prohibit (or restrict) new development in a floodplain or a watershed. It may impose special restrictions on devel-

23

opment in sensitive areas, such as wetlands, archaeological sites and historic districts.

If the land desired for a superstore is already zoned for large-scale commercial development, the developer has what is called "as-of-right" zoning and will not need to get the land rezoned. If the land is zoned for agricultural, industrial, or residential purposes, he will need a rezoning. The process for obtaining a rezoning is spelled out in the local zoning code. It usually requires public hearings and thus gives citizens an opportunity to comment. The burden of proof is on the person seeking a rezoning, not on the local city or county council. In other words, it is reasonable *and entirely legal* for the local government to deny a rezoning unless this burden of proof is met. If the developer simply seeks a minor adjustment to the zoning rules in order to build a project, he may still need to obtain a zoning "variance." Again, the criteria and procedures for approving variances are set forth in the local zoning code.

Rather than granting zoning approvals "as a matter of right," many localities use a special permitting process to regulate commercial devel-opment. (Other labels used for this process are "special exceptions," "special uses," or "conditional uses.") In these cases, specific land uses are often permitted so long as certain conditions are met. For example, the town may wish to limit a store's hours of operation, night lighting, the location of exits and entrances, or the design of the building itself. Citizens may not be able to block a project through these special permits, but often they can mitigate potentially harmful effects.

Site Plan Review. Most communities also require commercial projects to undergo a "site plan" review before a building permit may be issued. This review may occur as part of a special permitting process or separately. It enables jurisdictions to influence a project's design. The local planning board will focus on such matters as the placement of buildings and utilities, surface and groundwater drainage, water supply, access to the site, parking, loading, lighting, landscaping, noise control, environmental mitigation, and traffic control. Generally a planning board must approve the site plan if specific standards are met, but this review

Oregon's land-use law requires local governments to establish "Urban Growth Boundaries" as a means of containing sprawl. New growth may occur within the boundary but not outside it.

24

process does give citizens yet another opportunity to influence a project's design and character.

While standards governing site plan review vary widely, some jurisdictions require that environmental and historic preservation concerns be addressed at this stage. Examples of issues often considered include open space retention, conservation of significant natural and historic resources, tree preservation, screening of parking lots, construction of sidewalks and crosswalks, and building design. Even if site plan review standards do not address environmental concerns, it may be possible to deal with these issues under more general criteria or to persuade a developer to consider them on his own. This is especially true if citizens are vocal regarding a proposed project.[40]

The point is this: your zoning ordinance may offer useful hooks for fighting sprawl. These should be identified through a reading of the ordinance. As with the comprehensive plan, you should know what the ordinance says and doesn't say.

If you or your group can turn to a lawyer or planner for help in under-standing the ordinance, great. If not, you shouldn't hesitate to read the code yourself. Even if you don't understand everything, you can at least identify areas that warrant further research and then turn to appropriate experts for help in interpreting specific zoning provisions. If you are dissatisfied with the legal or other experts' response, question them further or get a second opinion.

Keep a record of any problems identified through this reading of the plan and zoning ordinance. When things settle down, you may want to push for revisions in these codes if they seem inadequate. Policies that promote sprawl or that expose important community assets to harmful development should be expunged.

If the ordinance does not require new commercial developments to fit in with the scale of the existing community, you may want to advocate a policy of requiring special reviews for developments over a certain size. For example, the Cape Cod (Mass.) Commission considers any retail or wholesale business greater than 10,000 square feet to be a "Development of Regional Impact" requiring special scrutiny.

State Laws

State Environmental Policy Acts. Most states have enacted state environmental policy acts. Generally modelled after the federal National Environmental Policy Act[41], these laws require state agencies, and in some states, local governments, to consider and minimize adverse environmental impacts caused by projects assisted through government grants, loans, licenses or permits. California and New York have perhaps the most effective state environmental laws. Impacts are typically disclosed through environmental assessments of large-scale developments. If an assessment shows that a project will harm the environment, the state may withhold its approval or require changes in the project to minimize the harm. Approval to build a major outlying shopping center might well be considered to have an adverse environmental impact. Connecticut, Indiana, Massachusetts, California, Montana, New York and Washington require that secondary and growth-inducing environmental impacts of proposed developments be considered.[42]

State Land-Use Planning Laws. Several states have enacted statewide

25

land-use planning and growth-management laws that give citizens a handle for controlling sprawl. These include Vermont, Maine, Maryland, Rhode Island, New Jersey, Florida, Georgia, Oregon, Hawaii, and Washington. States considering such legislation include California, Colorado, Pennsylvania, and Virginia. States with regional growth-management laws include New York (for the Adirondacks), Massachusetts (for Cape Cod), California (for the Lake Tahoe area and coastal zones), and North Carolina (for coastal zones).[43]

26 Most of these laws make it official state policy to channel new growth and development into existing cities and towns and away from the undeveloped countryside. Such policies reflect a desire not only to protect natural resources and farmland but also to reduce costs to the taxpayer of subsidizing inefficiently sited development. Washington state's growth management law, for example, calls for "[e]ncourag[ing] development in urban areas where adequate public facilities and services exist or can be provided in an efficient manner" and "[r]educing the inappropriate conversion of undeveloped land into sprawling, low-density development." Maryland's Resource Protection and

Planning Act of 1992 requires local planning commissions to follow the state's official policy of directing new growth into existing population centers. It also says state funds may not pay for local construction projects that undermine the town's comprehensive plan.

"Goal 14" of Oregon's land-use law requires local governments to establish "Urban Growth Boundaries." Under this concept, municipalities must calculate the amount of land needed for future growth and then draw a line around that acreage. New growth may occur within the line but not outside it. The boundary thus helps to contains sprawl.

In the 1980s citizens used Goal 14 to challenge a decision by the town of Jacksonville that would have promoted sprawl and weakened the downtown. When the town approved 700 acres of land for new growth, even though it needed only 96 acres, 1000 Friends of Oregon and local preservation advocates sued the town. In 1985, the Court of Appeals of the State of Oregon agreed that the city had drawn its urban growth boundary too generously.[44]

Vermont's Act 250, enacted in 1970, is intended to protect the state from costs associated with large-scale development that adversely affects scenic and historic resources, the environment, cities and towns, and the fiscal health of municipalities. This law asks such questions as:

• Does the proposed development conform with a community's vision for its own future, as expressed in land-use plans officially adopted by the citizenry's representatives?

• Will the development have an undue adverse effect on an area's scenic, natural, or historic sites? On the aesthetic quality of a community?

• Will the development cause an unreasonable burden on the ability of a municipality to provide government services?

• Will the development cause unreasonable highway congestion?

If a proposed development does not adequately address these concerns, Vermont's district environmental commissions may deny a development permit. Act 250 isn't perfect, but it is widely credited with having protected Vermont's towns and

Create a flow chart so you can visualize the entire development permitting process—and key deadlines for public comments—at a glance.

countryside against the sprawl that has made so much of America faceless.

Even states without growth-management laws have statutes available to fight sprawl. In Alabama, for example, the Downtown Redevelopment Authorities Act permits local redevelopment agencies to issue tax-exempt bonds to finance development projects that revive downtowns. When the town of Hamilton used this authority to finance a sprawling shopping center on farmland outside the downtown, a local business challenged this action in court. In an important ruling, the Supreme Court of Alabama held:

... there are 27 vacant buildings in the downtown area surrounding the Marion County Courthouse. This we find to be the precise sort of situation the legislature contemplated in enacting the [Downtown Redevelopment Authorities] Act. The legislature obviously intended to promote... revitalization of downtown central business districts that were once economically prosperous, but are in a state of decline and deterioration due to numerous reasons, one certainly being the development of shopping centers like the

one in this case that is located in the outlying areas of the city ...

The bonds that the Act empowered an authority to authorize...were not designed to develop projects located away from the central downtown business district, such as the shopping center in this case. These types of developments only provide more competition for the downtown area and further contribute to its decline; they certainly do not contribute to the "revitalization and redevelopment of the central business district."[45]

In other states, governors have issued executive orders directing state agencies to locate in older buildings downtown whenever possible. Vermont's Executive Order 15, for example, directs the Department of State Buildings to "give priority to locating state government activities in historic buildings." Massachusetts' Executive Order 134 declared it official state policy "to foster economic growth and development in downtown centers" and ordered state agencies to use space in existing buildings whenever possible or, when not possible, to build new buildings in the downtown.

The point is this: state laws often

27

contain useful provisions and policies for combatting sprawl. Citizens should acquaint themselves with these laws.[46]

Federal Laws

In general, most legal power for combatting sprawl resides with local or state governments. The federal government offers comparatively little assistance in this area. Even so, a few federal laws can help citizens in their battles against sprawl—and these laws can be used to educate local public officials about the long-term harm that sprawl can inflict on their community.

National Environmental Policy Act
The National Environmental Policy Act (NEPA) requires the preparation of an Environmental Impact Statement (EIS) for all "major federal actions significantly affecting the quality of the human environment."[47] Like Section 106 of the National Historic Preservation Act (discussed below), NEPA applies to federally funded projects and to private projects that require federal licenses or permits. Examples of federal involvement associated with sprawl include Army Corps of Engineers permits for filling wetlands under Section 404 of the Clean Water Act,[48] federal transportation funding for roads, and Housing and Urban Development (HUD) funds from Community Development Block Grants.

The environmental review under NEPA must precede issuance of the federal funding or permit. Often an Environmental Assessment (EA) will be made in order to determine whether the environmental impact of a project is significant, thereby warranting an EIS. An EIS must consider indirect impacts such as "growth inducing effects and other effects related to induced changes in the pattern of land use, population density or growth rate," along with alternatives to avoid these impacts. The environmental review must also consider impacts on "urban quality, historic and cultural resources, and the design of the built environment."

Section 106

Section 106 of the National Historic Preservation Act[49] requires federal agencies to consider the impact of their undertakings, including the provision of funding and the granting of a license, permit, or approval, on properties listed in or eligible for the National Register of Historic Places.

The Register is a roster of historically or architecturally significant sites. Before an agency begins the under-taking, it must consult with the state historic preservation office (SHPO) to identify such sites. If a federally-aided project—a highway or sewer line, for example—endangers these sites, the SHPO and the federal Advisory Council on Historic Preservation must be given an opportunity to recommend ways of mitigating the harm. Citizens groups may also have an opportunity to become involved in this process. If the agency, the SHPO, and the Advisory Council can reach an agreement on how best to mitigate the project's adverse effects, this agreement will be embodied in a legally-binding and enforceable "Memorandum of Agreement (MOA)." However, so long as federal agencies go through this "review and mitiga-tion" process, there is no requirement that they enter into such an agreement. They can proceed as they wish, even if that means the demoli-tion of historic properties.

Like NEPA, Section 106 is like a stop sign. It says to federal agencies: "Stop, look and listen before you rush ahead. Once you've done that, you are free to proceed as you please." Section 106 thus offers *procedural* rather than

28

substantive protection for historic and archaeological resources. However, by providing an opportunity for discussion of ways to mitigate a project's harm, Section 106 provides an opportunity to transform this procedural protection into substantive protection through an MOA. (See Appendix B for listing of SHPOs.)

Section 4(f)

Section 4(f) of The Department of Transportation Act[50] is, in some ways, stronger than Section 106. It says federally-aided transportation projects that would use historic sites, public parks, or wildlife refuges may not proceed unless there is *no feasible and prudent alternative*. If there is no such alternative, all possible planning must occur to minimize harm to affected sites. If, for example, a superstore requires the construction of new road lanes that are federally financed, and if the new lanes affect historic sites, public parks, or wildlife refuges, Section 4(f) may be invoked.

Unlike Section 106, Section 4(f) applies to historic sites designated by local and state governments as well as to National Register properties.

Transportation and the Clean Air Laws

The Intermodal Surface Transportation Efficiency Act (ISTEA) of 1991 and the Clean Air Act Amendments (CAAA) of 1990 have put new pressure on states and localities to reduce automobile dependence and to improve air quality. Because superstore sprawl works against these national objectives, citizens should familiarize themselves with these laws.

ISTEA prohibits the use of any federal funds for new "single-occupancy vehicle" highway lanes in areas that violate air quality standards (like most of New Jersey, much of California, and many metropolitan areas), unless such projects are linked to efforts to reduce traffic congestion. The Clean Air Act authorizes the withholding of federal highway funds to states that fail to meet clean air standards. In order to meet these requirements and avoid the loss of federal funds, states and localities will need to consider the effects of local zoning and development decisions on vehicular travel and air quality.

Because federal funds are often used to pay for highway improvements that serve superstores, citizens may find these ISTEA and CAAA requirements useful in opposing local zoning decisions that lead to dramatic increases in automotive traffic and air pollution. The preservation of walkable downtowns and the avoidance of auto-dependent sprawl should be considered a "transportation demand reduction strategy," as federal law puts it, for meeting ISTEA and CAAA requirements.[51]

Visualize the big picture. After you have identified all of the various permits and approvals that a proposed development will require, create a flow chart so you can visualize the overall process. You need to see at a glance when important hearings, deadlines for the submission of written comments, or other events occur. Include in the chart all opportunities for appeals and referendum petitions together with deadlines. It is easy to get caught up in the details of a controversy and to overlook the big picture.

29

This scene from downtown Holland, Michigan, illustrates an alternative to sprawl: a revitalized central business district. Private citizens, public officials, and businesses in Holland organized a Main Street program to strengthen the economic vitality and attractiveness of their downtown. See Chapter Twelve. (Photo: Riverview—Greg Holcombe)

Chapter Five

Grassroots Organizing

An overriding goal should be to generate broad-based public support for your campaign.

The policies discussed in Chapter Four can help in the fight against sprawl, but they are no substitute for organizing fellow citizens or winning public support for your efforts. Strong laws won't help very much if the public doesn't understand or support your objectives. An overriding goal should be to generate broad-based support for your campaign. Although land use and real estate development issues may be new to you, you can draw on your knowledge of techniques used to garner public support for other community causes, such as local bond issues or election campaigns. The broader and more diverse your base of support, the more likely you are to win. Steps you can take to build such support are outlined below.

Form a committee. First, if you have determined that a major grass-roots campaign is necessary in order to modify or stop sprawl-type development, recognize that you can't do everything yourself. You will need help. Talk to others in your community who may feel as you do, recruit some allies and form a committee. Then delegate responsibility. Put someone in charge of every major activity you anticipate carrying out. You may want to name special coordinators to handle fundraising, legal research, planning board liaison, volunteer recruitment and coordination, public testimony, media relations, newsletters, petitions, and other matters.

You should also pick a chairperson (or co-chairpersons). If you are opposing or trying to modify a certain type of development, it's good to select a businessperson rather than someone known primarily as an environmentalist or preservationist, if possible. In any event, the chair should be an articulate and highly motivated spokesperson who can lead and inspire others. Try to make your committee as broad-based as possible. Include people who are not only good workers but also have important expertise and relationships with key organizations. Involving a lawyer (preferably a volunteer) early in the process is wise.

Once formed, your committee should meet regularly. Each meeting should have an agenda, stay focused, and move forward. Meandering, unfocused meetings will frustrate supporters and cause them to drop out. You may want to invite grass-roots organizers from other communities—people who have already gone through the experience you now face—to speak to your committee.

Be sensitive to the roles that people can play and not play. Business people may support your effort but prefer to remain in the background for fear of alienating customers. Ask them to contribute funds or to talk one-on-one to local officials. At the same time, let merchants know that by speaking out publicly, they can help to generate valuable citizen support for the overall effort.

Choose a name for your group. Your group needs to establish an identity. Also, since it presumably will be sending out various communications, people will want to know their source. Give careful thought to the name. It should be brief but tell people immediately where you stand. "Citizens for Responsible Development" is an example of a name used by some local groups.

Develop a game plan. Think carefully about your objectives. Then develop a logical and comprehensive plan for achieving them. Update this plan as needed. Above all, *focus on priorities.* Make sure the most important actions receive adequate attention in a timely fashion. Establish a system for coordi-

nating activities, providing feedback, and ensuring appropriate follow-up.

Think about who in your community influences whom, about the power structure and relationships that govern the way things get done. What holes exist in your knowledge? How can you fill them? Who should call whom? What points should be made by those assigned to make key calls? Are there organizational boards (or board members) who should be contacted? In short, make effective use of your community's existing power structure as much as possible.

Develop a public position statement. Think through all of the reasons to be concerned about the proposed development. Identify the ways you think it should be modified (or opposed altogether). Do the necessary research to back up any arguments you need to make. Then develop a position statement. Keep it simple and concise but make it compelling.

Educate key policymakers and local opinion leaders. Identify and then seek to educate council members who are still neutral or undecided regarding the proposed development. Use peer contacts to reach these

Think carefully about your objectives. Then develop a logical and comprehensive plan for achieving them. Focus on priorities.

32

"We're Against Sprawl Committee" 8-Week Campaign Plan

members as well as key civic and business leaders.

Strategize with people on your side. If individual town council members or other key citizens seem sympathetic to your position, seek their advice on where to focus your efforts, which questions to research, which of their peers are "persuadable," which ones are "hopeless."

Organize public testimony. Remember, it's easier to nip a bad idea in the bud than to fight it in full bloom. This may involve testifying against the super-sprawl proposal while it is still under review by the local planning commission and before it goes to the full governing body.

Recruit people to speak out at public hearings. Most zoning ordinances require hearings on proposed rezonings (and on special exceptions and zoning variances) and again later on specific site plans. The hearings enable you to educate local public officials, journalists, and the public. This is especially true if the hearings are covered by cable TV.

Think carefully about the most important points to make at these hearings and about who would be

Timeline	Item
	Organizational Matters
August 9	a. Open bank account
	b. Accept donations
	c. Appoint treasurer and steering committee of at least 5 persons
	Grassroots Deliverables
August 30	• 500 Bumperstickers "We're Against Sprawl" on cars
August 23 to Referendum Day	• Referendum work Identify 1,000 voters & GOTV calls day before and on voting day
September 20 through Referendum Day	• Letters to the Editor (minimum of 50) Find volunteers to write
4-5 days before vote	• Literature drop 5,000 pieces or insert
8 days before vote	• Dear Friends post cards: 2,000 Identify 40 volunteers to write 50 friends each
1 week before referendum	• Special event: Walk Against Sprawl
	Media Deliverables
1 week before referendum	• 3-4 full page newspaper ads: 21" deep by 10-3/10" wide. Newspaper (full page by 5 columns)
8 days before referendum	• 30 second radio spots (4 rotation): minimum of 60 spots. 6 per day, building to 10 per day. Use local celebrity voice ads.
6-8 days before vote	• Mini ads: Why I'm Against Sprawl signed ads. 24 total.

33

This anti-sprawl campaign plan is a modification of the plan prepared by Al Norman for Greenfield, Massachusetts' "We're Against the Wal Committee." See Chapter 9.

your best spokesperson. Often it is useful to recruit several speakers, with each one making a different point. Avoid a line-up of witnesses who simply rehash what each other says. Statements should be brief and concise. You don't want to waste time by droning on repetitiously, although key points should be reinforced. If many people want to speak but there isn't enough time, they can wear badges or buttons to the hearing and communicate their feelings that way.

Turn out for hearings. Encourage people to show up in force for the public hearings. Even if they don't testify, their presence in the audience will let public officials know the citizenry takes the issue seriously and wants it handled well. It will also give your side a better understanding of specific questions individual policy-makers may have. You can then answer these questions in follow-up meetings, letters or testimony. It's good to have the hearing room filled when the planning board (or city/county council) actually votes on a proposal, even if the vote doesn't occur until midnight.

To find out when the hearings are scheduled, you can check the newspaper, of course, but hearing

notices are usually buried and easy to overlook. Many planning depart-ments have special mailing lists for citizens who want to be notified of public hearings on zoning matters. See if this is the case in your community and get on the list. You should also check periodically with the planning board staff on the status of hearings. Ideally, you will have someone in your group in charge of liaison with the planning staff. That person should keep close tabs on hearing dates.

Request an independent analysis of the proposed development's effects. Given the major and long-term impact that a superstore is likely to have on your community, it is reason-able to ask your local officials to make decisions in as informed a way as possible. Ask the town council to commission an independent fiscal/economic/traffic/environ-mental analysis of the proposed devel-opment. Questions that might appropriately be raised in this context include the following:

• What are the size and characteris-tics of the present and potential trade market areas for the proposed development?

• What are the projected annual sales of the superstore? What percentage of the area's total retail market does this represent?

• To what extent will the superstore and spin-off development expand the retail market or simply redistribute existing consumer spending?

• What types of businesses will be attracted by the superstore?

• What is the potential for losses among existing retailers in terms of sales and jobs as a result of the new superstore? Have long-term as well as short-term losses been considered?

• What effect will the superstore likely have on vacancies in downtown buildings and reduced tax assess-ments resulting from vacancies?

• How many new jobs will be generated by the new superstore? How many will be lost by displaced businesses? How do the jobs in each category compare in terms of wages and benefits?

• What will it cost the municipality to provide (*and maintain over time*) the new development with public services and infrastructures? What will it cost the state to build and maintain new roads?[52]

In many cases, local governments have asked developers (or their partner superstores) to pay for these studies. Depending on local circumstances, this may be reasonable. However, work to ensure that a fair-minded town official is the one to formulate the assumptions, shape the questions, select whoever conducts the study, and generally maintain control.

One word of caution: *Don't ask* for a development impact analysis if you have reason to question the town's ability to ensure a high-quality job or its willingness to ensure that important issues receive fair consideration. (Getting an inadequate study done could actually set your effort back.) In this case, consider having your citizens' organization commission its own analysis. Make sure the person selected to conduct this research is well-respected and understands all the issues involved.

Ask for more time when necessary. Sometimes what you most need is simply more time—time to gather information, time for people to read and digest it. Consider asking the planning (or town) board to defer

critical votes if important information has not yet been gathered and analyzed. Above all, guard against being pressured to rush a development proposal through without a thorough review of all the fiscal, environmental, and economic impacts. Proponents of sprawl will give all sorts of reasons for racing ahead. But remember: your community will have to live with (and possibly pay for) any negative impacts for a very long time.

Tap available talent and information. Make good use of whatever talent and expertise exists in your community. This may come from local or regional planning, environmental, business or other groups. It may come from the League of Women Voters. Or it may come from local universities, which often have business, planning, environmental and other departments. University professors can sometimes help with research, expert testimony, and the like.

If you want to find out about a certain corporation and its effects on other communities, go to the local library and get a computerized list of news articles on the company. Then track down the articles and read them.

Circulate petitions. As momentum

Numbers and dry test can make peoples' eyes glaze over. Enliven the presentation of your information with pictures, graphics, and other visual aids.

35

builds in your cause's favor, you may want to initiate a petition to let public officials know how many people want the proposed development modified or rejected. If the petition forms include a space for telephone numbers in addition to petitioners' names and addresses, you can use these numbers later to turn people out for future activities. Bring your petition forms to major community gatherings. It's easier to get people to sign up in large numbers that way.

Use visuals. Numbers and dry text can make peoples' eyes glaze over. Enliven the presentation of your information with visual aids. Opponents of sprawl in Greenfield, Mass., prepared a drawing showing that one superstore alone would exceed the total square footage of the entire downtown.

Prepare fliers. Most people won't (or can't) take the time to plow through turgid economic, environmental and traffic-impact studies. Synthesize the important information found in such studies, then break it up and present it in a digestible form, something the average citizen can read quickly and understand. Consider distributing fliers—especially if your local paper refuses to publish important informa-

36

tion. Let people know how to contact key public officials to express their opinions.

Be visible. Let people know that opponents of sprawl have a chance of winning. Hope and optimism are key to keeping spirits up and momentum going. Making your point of view visible helps. Distribute bumper stickers, fliers, buttons and T-shirts with your slogan printed on them. Sell these items if possible to raise money for necessary expenses.

Write letters to decisionmakers. Make sure your local policymakers have the information they need to make informed decisions. Letters sent to decisionmakers should be as thoughtful and concise as possible. They should never be disrespectful or intimidating.

Raise money. You will need to pay for phone calls, photocopying, supplies, bumper stickers, badges, legal counsel and other expenses. Depending on how much coverage you can generate in your local media, you may also need to pay for radio spots and newspaper ads. Create a fundraising committee comprised of three or four people who are good at raising money and willing to commit

Don't let anyone tell you that sprawl is inevitable . . . The biggest enemy is a sense of hopelessness.

the necessary time to it. The committee should identify local merchants, organizations and individuals with a major stake in the outcome of your campaign. A basic principle of fundraising is that people give money to people as much as to causes, so be sure to identify the right person to contact these groups or individuals. Once your prospects are identified, go after them.

You can also provide contribution forms for people to fill out and return in your fliers, newspaper ads, and other materials.

A common problem is the feeling among small businesses that protecting their business is anti-competitive. Bear in mind that the superstores have available and often spend large sums of money in their efforts to secure rezonings, win referenda, or otherwise influence local decisions. As one citizen activist put it, "It's ridiculous for small businesses not to make an investment in their own future. If the big corporations are spending money, small businesses should be willing to protect their investments. The 'bake sale' mentality won't cut it. You have to fight capital with capital."

1. Obtain a copy of the developer's proposal and analyze it.

2. Find out if the proposed development complies with relevant federal, state and local laws.

3. Make a flow chart of the development review process and include time deadlines.

4. Think your objectives through carefully and set priorities.

5. Organize a committee and delegate responsibility.

6. Develop a well-reasoned position on the proposed development and back up your position with careful research.

7. Develop grass-roots organizing and media strategies.

8. Generate letters to the editor and opinion pieces in the local paper early.

9. Meet with local officials and opinion leaders. Draw their attention to facts they need to know.

10. Turn out and speak out at public hearings.

11. Ask the city council to analyze the development's probable fiscal, economic, environmental, traffic and other impacts. Make sure long-term impacts are considered.

12. Circulate petitions.

13. Distribute simple fliers clearly summarizing your position and the reasons for it.

14. Raise money to pay for radio spots, newspaper ads, bumper stickers, and other ways of getting your message across.

15. Above all, build broad public support for your position. Work to reach different segments of the community, especially local business and civic leaders.

37

Be sure to find out about and comply with any relevant state or local laws regarding any fundraising or political activities in which you may engage.

Write the board of directors of the superstore corporation. The boards of many national corporations are insulated from the negative impacts of their corporation's activities. If you are getting nowhere with your local public officials, the developer, and the corporation's regional representatives, write directly to the corporation's board members. You can obtain a list of board members simply by writing (or calling) the public affairs office at corporate headquarters and requesting a copy of the corporation's annual report.

Don't get discouraged. It is easy to get demoralized during these battles. There will surely be moments when you will feel the odds are overwhelming. Don't let dejection take over and don't let anyone tell you that sprawl is inevitable. Most victories over superstore sprawl involve major setbacks along the way. Some campaigns take a long time. But losing one battle is not losing the war. (See Chapter 9.)

Believe that you can make a difference. Believe in yourself and in the power of citizen action. It's amazing how much an individual or a small group of committed volunteers can accomplish. Many organizations that turn out to have a real impact spring from the leadership of just one or two people. The biggest enemy is a sense of hopelessness. Often hundreds (or even thousands) of people will stew silently over the same problem but think that nothing they can do as individuals will make a difference. Somebody needs to light the match.

Never doubt that a few committed individuals can change the world. Indeed, it is the only thing that ever has.
—Margaret Mead

38

Chapter Six   Media Strategies

Having done all this community organizing, how will you tell people what you seek to accomplish and why? After all, it doesn't do much good to take all these steps if no one knows about your activities. It is critical to understand and work with the media in order to get your message out to the community as a whole and to build the broad-based public support so essential to your success.

Match your media strategy to your overall strategy. The media offer a tool for communicating your messages and points of view. They are not an end in and of themselves. To use the media to your advantage, it's important to have a clearly defined comprehensive strategy. Make sure you can answer the following questions: What do you wish to accomplish? How will you achieve your goals? Who are your allies? Your opponents? Whom are you trying to reach with your point of view? What is the best way to reach those individuals or groups? Do you have all the facts together to support your position?

Once you have mapped out your overall strategy, you can carry out an appropriate media strategy.

Define your message and audience. The first step of your media strategy should be to determine what you want to say (messages) and to whom you want to say it (target audiences). It's helpful to develop three or four key points (more than that is hard for people to absorb) that you and your group wish to make and then to communicate those points in all your activities, not just with the media.

Once you have defined your messages, you can then determine which media outlets reach targetted constituencies. Make a list of newspapers, television stations, magazines and newsletters you consider appropriate. Public libraries often contain directories of media outlets. Newsrooms are notorious for high turnover, so make sure you call and find out which editor or reporter covers a particular issue before sending a press release or invitation to an event.

Identify key spokespersons. Designate two or three people as your official spokespersons with the press. These people should be the only ones who speak with reporters and editors. Limiting the number of people who talk to the press helps to ensure that your group consistently says the same thing. Nothing can be worse than for

one member of your group to say something only to be contradicted by another member. Make sure those designated as spokespersons have all the facts and feel comfortable in dealing with the press.

Communicate with the Media on Their Terms

Press releases. Typically the best way to let the press know who you are and what you are doing is to send a press release. Press releases should be no longer than two pages and should include a contact name, a telephone number, and a release date for the information. Key information—who, what, where, when, and why—should appear in the first couple of paragraphs. Reporters and editors are always trying to meet tight deadlines. Don't make them work for the information.

Letters to the editor/op-ed pieces. Writing letters to the editor and opinion pieces for local newspapers can help generate awareness of your group and your issues. It's important to let others in the community who share your concerns know they are not alone. It's also good to get your views in print early enough to influence the debate—before key decisions are locked in. Persuade others to send letters as well. Typically, opinion pieces are approximately 750-800 words in length. Call the editors of the daily and weekly papers in your area to find out what length they prefer. Try to time the placement of your piece around an upcoming event, such as a public hearing on the issue. Having a well-known member of the community author the op-ed piece strengthens the prospects for its placement. Many people will think, "If so-and-so is concerned, perhaps I should be, too."

40 Once letters are printed, you can copy and "recycle" them into information packets that continue to circulate. These packets offer an efficient way to educate the public and the media. When you copy, don't make the letters so small that people have difficulty reading them. Presentation is important. It may also be useful to copy the letters onto 8-1/2" x 11" paper so they can be easily recopied or faxed.

Fact sheets/position papers. It's helpful to prepare fact sheets and brief position papers outlining your group and your point of view. These can be left with a reporter after an interview or handed out to the press covering a public hearing or an event. Be sure to make your key points in these materials.

Phone calls. Try to get to know the reporters who cover your area and issue. Call the reporter and tell him or her about your group and upcoming events and offer to send a press release or other relevant materials. Some words of caution: make sure the reporter is not on deadline when you call, be brief, have all the facts at hand, and don't be a pest. In all your communications, speak in plain English. Use colorful language and metaphors. When preparing materials, tell your story as if you were talking with a friend or relative.

Organize newsworthy events. When planning an event or preparing testimony, consider how newsworthy it is. News organizations are concerned with the present and the future. They are not interested in the testimony you gave last week or the protest you staged a month ago unless it is to provide background for the event you will hold tomorrow.

The question you must answer is: Why should anyone care? Other factors that might make your work newsworthy: Is it the first time certain community groups have come together to work on an issue? Is there an unusual partnership between business and environmental groups? Is there a well-known community leader or celebrity who either is a part of your group or will be attending the event? Do you have new and interesting research to report? Are you using unusual strategies to make your points? Do you have results from a recent public opinion survey to report?

The list of possible media events is endless. Panel discussions, community marches, candelight parades, and skits are events some communities have organized with positive results. Others have invited effective and knowledgeable speakers to address key local groups—e.g., chambers of commerce, Leagues of Women Voters, city/county councils, planning boards and other groups.

Tips for Dealing with Print Reporters

• Unless the reporter conducts an in-depth profile, you will most likely be answering questions over the phone rather than in a face-to-face interview. It is not necessary to respond the instant a reporter calls. Find out what

Prepare fact sheets and brief position papers outlining your point of view. These can be left with a reporter after an interview or handed out to the press covering a public hearing.

his or her deadline is and promise to get back. By so doing, you will have time to think about your position and organize your facts. Try to respect the reporter's deadline, however.

• Make sure the reporter knows where you can be reached in case additional information is needed after your interview.

• Don't panic if the reporter uses a tape recorder. It can improve your chances of being quoted accurately.

• You may talk with a reporter for an hour only to find that you are quoted briefly or not at all. Don't get discouraged or angry. While you may not be quoted directly, your information probably helped to shape the story.

• Never ask to read the reporter's copy or request changes before publication.

• If you feel you are misquoted or there are gross inaccuracies in the story printed, call the reporter and ask for a correction. If the reporter doesn't respond, contact his editor. If that fails, write a letter to the editor for publication.

• Don't complain about minor slips in an otherwise accurate story.

Complaining over minor matters can antagonize the reporter.

• If you are trying to persuade the reporter to do a story, remember to:

• Call when the reporter is not on deadline. Always ask if you don't know when the deadlines are. If it's a bad time, call back.

• Do your homework. Find out which reporters cover particular topics. Nothing is more frustrating to a harried reporter than to have someone call pitching a story on commercial development when that reporter covers health care.

• Have the facts about your story. If you are pitching an event you plan to hold, know where and when it will be and be able to explain why it is significant.

Tips for dealing with Broadcast Interviews

For both radio and TV interviews:

• Assume that you are on the air until you are told otherwise. Nothing could be worse than to make an embarrassing remark such as "I'm glad that ordeal is over" and then discover that

41

the tape is still running or the "on-air" light is still on.

For TV interviews:

• Don't make unnecessary movements and noises. Not only are quick body and hand movements hard for the camera to follow, they can make you look nervous, awkward, and defensive.

• Sit erect and lean slightly forward in your chair to convey confidence and control of the situation. Take care not to slouch or be too casual in your sitting posture.

• Think in sound bites: use short, catchy phrases to make your points. Avoid jargon and long sentences.

• Act as though you are on camera at all times. Directors often will keep you on camera while the host or another guest is speaking to capture your reactions.

• You want to be remembered for what you have to say, not for what you are wearing. Choose solid colors and pastel shades or off-white for shirts and blouses. Avoid large prints or patterns; black and white or shiny fabrics; noisy jewelry or loose change

in pockets. Women should wear street make-up.

For radio interviews:

• Maintain a distance of six to eight inches from the microphone, with elbows on the table.

• Speak normally. Shouting is unnecessary as the microphone is very sensitive.

• Avoid noisy jewelry and loose change in pockets.

• Use short sentences and speak clearly and concisely. Remember there will be no visuals to back you up.

This chapter on media strategies was written by Elizabeth L. Wainger, director for public affairs, National Trust for Historic Preservation.

1. Know thy objective/know thy message. *This sounds obvious but you must have a very clear idea of what you want to communicate and say it. Before the interview, ask yourself: What are our key objectives? What do I want the press coverage to do for me?*

2. Know thy reporter. *When a reporter calls, you don't have to respond immediately. Find out what the reporter wants and then call back. This gives you some time to think about your response. However, make sure you find out what the reporter's deadline is and respond in a timely fashion.*

3. Know thy medium. *Reporters, especially television and radio reporters, work under tight deadlines. They need answers fast. They also need short answers. A TV news story may be only a minute or two long. In that minute you may be quoted for only 10 seconds. So there is no time to beat around the bush. You've got to make your point quickly and clearly. You want to give the reporter what he needs (so he'll use it), but in a way that is beneficial to you. Respect the reporter's deadlines.*

42

4. Know thy audience. *Before talking to the press, think about who will be reached by the article or TV/radio program. If it's a local paper or TV station, the audience will be a broad cross-section of the general public. Before the interview, think about why the reader (or viewer) care about your issue.*

5. Thou shalt make a list of key points. *Again, before the interview, make a list of key points you want to communicate. Write them down. You probably don't go to the super-market without a list. How can you expect to remember everything you want to say in a high-pressure situation such as an interview? Figure out three to five main points and refer to them throughout the interview.*

6. Thou shalt not use jargon. *Use words that the audience can under-stand or else you are not communi-cating. Translate technical jargon into plain English.*

7. Thou shalt not go off the record. *Everything you say to a reporter can and will be used against you. Consider that the reporter is taking notes from the moment you answer the phone until you hang up.*

8. Thou shalt not make off-the-cuff remarks. *Never say anything that you wouldn't want on the front page of the* New York Times *or your local paper. Weigh your words carefully.*

9. Thou shalt not lie. *Lying to or misleading someone can severely damage your credibility. If you don't know the answer to a question, say so. If you can't comment on something, say so. Don't get defensive. Just be firm.*

10. Thou shalt not say "no comment." *There are other ways to tell a reporter that you will not answer a question: "It really would not be appropriate or responsible for me to answer that at this time;" or "Until we have more information, it is inappropriate for me to comment on the situation."*

11. Thou shalt not repeat a negative question or phrase. *A reporter asks, "Isn't it true that preservationists are enemies of economic develop-ment?" Whatever you do, don't answer by repeating the phrase, such as "No, it is not true that preservationists are enemies of economic development." Take a less defensive, more positive stance. For example, you might say: "We believe*

preservation can actually stimulate economic growth." Then explain why and how.

12. Thou shalt not get angry. *No matter what happens, do not lose your cool. When you do that, reporters gain ratings points. Even worse, people remember simply that you got angry, not the important things you said.*

13. Thou shalt be yourself. *You are an individual, not a group. Even though you speak for your group, you are still an individual. So don't use the "we" word. It's better to say "I think" or "I do not know," etc. Speak in personal terms to enhance credi-bility and reduce stuffiness.*

14. Thou shalt repeat your key points. *Sum up your key points briefly.*

Chapter Seven

The "Property Rights" Issue

The "property rights" issue often surfaces in debates over superstore sprawl. Proponents of unlimited development state the issue in various ways. Here are some common lines:

• The Founding Fathers of America would be horrified today if they saw how modern land-use restrictions interfere with personal property rights.

• Refusal to approve a proposed development violates the Fifth Amendment to the Constitution and is an illegal "taking" of private property.

• Any time a government takes an action that reduces the value of private property, it commits an unconstitutional "taking" and must compensate the property owner for any loss in property value caused by the governmental action.

• It's unconstitutional to prevent a property owner from using his property exactly as he pleases.

• If the local government does not approve a requested rezoning (or site plan), it can be taken to court and have to pay damages to the property owner. Are local taxpayers willing to risk this outcome?

• Maybe it was once accepted that local governments can regulate land in ways that incidentally affected private property values, but the *Lucas* (or *First English* or *Nollan*) decisions issued by the U. S. Supreme Court changed all that. The rules are different now.

The Founding Fathers and the Fifth Amendment

A good place to start disentangling the misunderstandings reflected by these statements is with the Fifth Amendment of the U.S. Constitution itself. This is the source of the concept of a "taking": a governmental action that so deprives a property owner of his land as to require monetary compensation. The "Just Compensation Clause" of the Fifth Amendment says:

nor shall private property be taken *[emphasis added] for public use, without just compensation.*

When Congress recommended in 1789 that the states approve these words as part of the Bill of Rights, it sought to protect American citizens from the physical seizure (or "taking") of private property by government. Before the Revolution, British soldiers could forcibly enter a person's property and take private property—food, animals, or lodging—without paying for it. The former colonists resented such heavy-handedness and wanted to guard against it in the new republic. Thus the Fifth Amendment's "Takings Clause" was intended to protect individual property owners against the physical taking of private property.

Regulatory Takings

It was not until 1922 that the concept of a "regulatory taking" took hold in American law. That year the U.S. Supreme Court held, in *Pennsylvania Coal v. Mahon,*[54] that if a government regulation goes "too far," it will be considered a "taking" requiring the payment of "just compensation." The court did not say what "too far" was. The meaning of those two little words remains the subject of heated debate today, 70 years later.

Compensation Is Not Required Just Because Regulations Affect Property Values

While introducing the concept of a

When one person's use of private land threatens to violate the rights of adjoining property owners or to harm the public health, safety, or general welfare, it is the duty of goverment to intervene.

regulatory vs. a *physical* "taking" to American law, the *Pennsylvania Coal* decision also made it clear that the government does not have to compensate landowners every time it takes an action affecting property values. As the court stated:

Government hardly could go on if to some extent values incident to property could not be diminished without paying for every such change in the general laws.

Since *Pennsylvania Coal* was handed down, the courts have frequently upheld government regulations that incidentally reduced private property values when such regulations were necessary to protect the public health, safety or general welfare. In doing so, courts have noted that, while their own property may be regulated, landowners claiming that a taking has occurred may also benefit from restrictions placed on others in their community.

Land-Use Regulations Are A Proper and Necessary Role of Government

It is perfectly lawful, and not unconstitutional, for government to prevent a property owner from using his property in certain ways as long as the government does so for the purpose of protecting the public health, safety, or general welfare and doesn't prevent the owner from using the property altogether. When one person's use of private land threatens to violate the rights of adjoining property owners or to harm the public health, safety, or general welfare, it is, in fact, the *duty* of government to intervene. That's partly why citizens create governments: to mediate competing rights as fairly and as wisely as possible. It is why zoning laws, which routinely curtail individual rights in favor of the public interest, sprang into existence decades ago.[55]

In the context of superstore sprawl, the developer's "right" to build on his land may affect an entire community's drinking water supply if oil run-off from surface parking, or chemicals sold in a garden center, are not handled properly. This "right" may lower the value of nearby homes purchased by people who reasonably assumed that the area would remain peaceful and attractive. Traffic brought by the new development may pollute the air or damage crops raised by local farmers. In short, one person's "right" to use land may be an infringement on someone else's right.

In general, government regulations that incidentally reduce the value of private property do not require compensation to affected property owners when such regulations:

• promote a valid public purpose, such as protection of the public health, safety, or general welfare; and

• leave the property owner with a reasonable economic use of the property.

It is, of course, also essential that government regulations comply with relevant state laws and respect the "due process" rights of citizens. Among other things, that means holding fair hearings, providing adequate public notice of governmental actions as well as avenues for appealing decisions. Basic fairness should underlie all governmental actions, regardless of what the courts require.

There is no real basis for the oft-made assertion that the Founding Fathers would have disapproved of modern land-use regulations that restrict what people can do with their property. On the contrary, it is highly questionable that the Founding Fathers would have countenanced

actions by private property owners that harmed the property rights of their neighbors or the well-being of the community as a whole. As George Washington wrote when he transmitted the Constitution to Congress in 1787:

Individuals entering into society must give up a share of liberty to preserve the rest.

And as Thomas Jefferson wrote regarding a property owner's claim to soil deposits along the Mississippi River:

[D]oes not common sense, the foundation of all authorities, of the laws themselves, and of their construction, declare it impossible that ... a single individual should have a lawful right to drown the city of New Orleans, or to injure, or change, of his own authority, the course or current of a river which is to give outlet to the productions of two thirds of the whole area of the United States?[56]

A Difference between Reasonable and Highest Economic Uses

Leaving an owner with a "reasonable economic use" of his property, as required by the courts, is quite

Property owners are not entitled to compensation for making bad business decisions.

46

different from guaranteeing someone the right to make the highest possible profit. Property owners sometimes assume they are entitled to maximum profits from their land. This is not the case. A homeowner living in a quiet neighborhood zoned for residential purposes is not legally entitled to sell his property for use as a convenience store, even though selling out to a convenience store chain might bring a much higher financial return. Neither is the local government required to rezone this person's land from residential to commercial purposes just to accommodate his desire to maximize profits. Yet this very type of argument is often used by landowners in rural areas to pressure local governments to rezone for commercial purposes land zoned for agricultural, residential or industrial uses. It is not uncommon for some people to argue, in effect, that government has an obligation to indulge their desire to profit from real estate speculation, even if such indulgence alters the entire community's way of life or vision for its future. But as the U.S. Supreme Court explained in *Penn Central Transportation Co. v. New York City:*

. . . the submission that [property owners] may establish a "taking"

simply by showing that they have been denied the ability to exploit a property interest that they heretofore had believed was available for development is quite simply untenable.[57]

People are not entitled to compensation for making bad business decisions. As the Supreme Court said in *Keystone Bituminous Coal Association* v. *DeBenedictis:*

That private individuals erred in taking a risk cannot estop the [State] from exercising its police power to abate activity akin to a public nuisance.[58]

In other words, the misjudgments of individuals should not prevent government from doing its job.

In general, property owners are entitled to use their land for the purposes for which it is zoned, provided they adhere to all applicable government regulations and do not harm their neighbors. But the government may legally alter the zoning, even if this means lowering land values at some point in the future, if it does so to protect the public health, safety, or general welfare and leaves property owners with a reasonable economic use of their land. As the

U.S. District Court for the Eastern District of New York put it in *Elias* v. *Town of Brookhaven:*[59]

If there is anything that the history of zoning regulation has established it is that as time passes and population increases (or diminishes) zoning restrictions change.

The Fifth Amendment itself does not guarantee to an investor in land that the existing zoning regulation will remain unchanged. . . To hold otherwise would be to draw into question the effective power of a locality to plan for the future needs of its citizens. Nor does the loss of profit or of the right to make the most profitable use of the property constitute a taking.

First English, Nollan and Lucas

In recent years, some people have begun to argue that the rules for land-use regulation have changed with the Supreme Court's *First English, Nollan,* and *Lucas* decisions. Since these cases are often misinterpreted, let's look at them briefly.

In *First English Evangelical Lutheran Church* v. *County of Los Angeles,*[60] a 1987 case, the Supreme Court held that *if* a government regulation were

47

found to be a taking because it denied a landowner *all* reasonable use or return from his property, the government *could* be required to pay monetary damages. This decision did not change the standard for a "taking," to wit, the denial of all reasonable economic use of private property. It simply said that if a regulatory taking does occur, even temporarily, the *remedy* may be financial compensation. Before *First English*, some courts had ruled that the government could simply invalidate the offending regulation; now it may have to pay cash.

In *Nollan* v. *California Coastal Commission*,[61] the Supreme Court ruled that there must be a reasonable link between a government regulation and its purpose. Such a "nexus," as the court put it, was found lacking in the commission's requirement that a beachfront property owner grant an easement along the shore so that the public could view the beach from the road above the owner's house.

At the same time, the *Nollan* decision reaffirmed the right of government to regulate land:[62]

We have long recognized that land-use regulation does not effect a taking if it

"substantially advance[s] legitimate state interests" and does not "den[y] an owner economically viable use of his land."

In *Lucas* v. *South Carolina Coastal Council*,[63] the court ruled that if a government regulation destroys "all economically beneficial or productive use" of one's land, the regulation will be considered a "taking" for which the government must compensate the property owner for any property value lost due to the regulation—unless the proposed land use is so harmful as to constitute a public "nuisance," in which case the landowner is not entitled to compensation. The *Lucas* decision is generally viewed as an extremely narrow one applicable to the rare situation in which a regulation totally destroys a property's value. Indeed, the Supreme Court itself described such cases as extremely rare.

What citizens should also know is that the *Lucas* decision quoted *Penn Central* favorably, thereby signalling that the court continues to recognize that government may implement land-use regulations to uphold the public interest in health, safety, and general welfare.

In *Concrete Pipe and Products of California* v. *Construction Laborers Pension Trust for Southern California*,[64] the Supreme Court rejected the argument that property owners can divide their property into segments and then claim compensation for regulated segments:

While Concrete Pipe tries to shoehorn its claim into this analysis by asserting that "[t]he property of [Concrete Pipe] which is taken, is taken in its entirety," ... we rejected this analysis years ago in Penn Central Transportation Co. *v.* New York City ... *where we held that a claimant's parcel of property could not first be divided into what was taken and what was left for the purpose of demonstrating the taking of the former to be complete and hence compensable. To the extent that any portion of property is taken, that portion is always taken in its entirety; the relevant question, however, is whether the property is taken is all, or only a portion of the parcel in question.*

The Fairness Issue

So much for the courts. There are also other responses to bogus "property rights" arguments trotted out in the guise of "freedom," "The American Way," and similar rhetoric.

Much of the value of an individual piece of land derives not from the property owner's investments or labor but from other property owners' work and public investments.[65] Public investments—roads, sewer lines, schools, libraries, police protection, etc.—contribute significantly to the value of private properties. If a property owner claims a "taking" when government refuses to inflate the value of his land with a rezoning, will he offer to reimburse the government when it adds value to his land by building roads? Hardly.

Property owners have the right to use their land in ways that do not harm others. As citizens of their community, they have a responsibility to respect the rights of others, including those of future generations.

Finally, as the Supreme Court observed in its 1987 *Keystone* decision, even though government regulations restrict individuals, they benefit people as well:[66]

Under our system of government, one of the state's primary ways of preserving the public weal is restricting the uses individuals can make of their property. While each of us is burdened somewhat by such restrictions, we, in turn, benefit greatly from the restrictions that are placed on others.[67]

Public investments—roads, sewer lines, schools, libraries, police protection, etc.— contribute significantly to the value of private property.

49

*Artwork for campaign buttons used by
Westford citizens battling a superstore.
(Artwork by Jonatha P. Walker-Rohs)*

Chapter Eight

Biting Down Like a Bulldog: Westford, Massachusetts

Part Three:

Case Studies and Better Models

The case of Westford, Massachusetts, illustrates the value of individual leadership and broad-based participation in the democratic system. It also shows that a few citizens who feel strongly can, with organization and commitment, effectively mobilize an entire town to defend its way of life. What occurred in Westford represents all that can happen when citizens take full advantage of the democratic process and media opportunities available to them.

Westford is a small, traditional New England town of 17,500 in northeastern Massachusetts with only one traffic light. The story here began on April 8, 1993, when the *Westford Eagle* announced that Wal-Mart planned a 161,267-square-foot superstore on the edge of Westford. The proposed superstore, three satellite stores, and a 944-space parking lot would spread over 25.2 acres.

Elizabeth Michaud read the story and felt unsettled by the prospect of Westford's suddenly becoming a regional shopping center. After stewing for two weeks over the impact of the new store, she decided to act. A technical writer, Michaud had no background whatsoever in land-use planning or real estate development issues.

The Westford land eyed for the superstore was already commercially zoned, which meant opponents of the project would not be able to stop the superstore by blocking a request for rezoning. They would have to take a different approach. One of Michaud's friends suggested she initiate a petition to demonstrate public opposition to the project. This struck Michaud as a sensible approach. With the annual town meeting already set for May 8, why not inaugurate the petition campaign the day of the meeting?

To jump-start the petition effort, Michaud submitted a guest editorial to the *Westford Eagle* two days before the town meeting. Here she publicly announced the petition drive and made her pitch.

These developers will pay attention to aesthetics and traffic and our feelings just enough so that they can come into our town, make their bundle, and leave us with the traffic, the ugliness, and a little spare change. We can give up, lie down, and let these developers steamroller right over us or we can stand up and fight for the quality of life in our town.[68]

Michaud emphasized that the project was not a foregone conclusion and urged people to call town planning board members and local selectmen. She also told people where they could sign petitions.

The day of the town meeting, Michaud and her allies garnered 300 signatures. At an early stage in the battle, then, the petition helped raise public awareness and provided concrete documentation of citizen opposition to the project. As Michaud would say later, "You can't argue with piles of signatures."

Meanwhile, the book club to which Michaud belongs supported her idea of ordering T-shirts to lend visibility to the budding opposition movement. With the help of her husband and using their computer, Michaud designed the shirt graphics. Within a few days, a local printer produced 48 red shirts with "STOP Wal-Mart" printed across the front. People wore these the day of the town meeting. Proceeds from the T-shirt sales provided seed money for campaign activities.

It took Michaud three weeks to realize she would need more help, so she recruited a few friends and formed the "STOP Wal-Mart Committee," with herself as chairman. A month later

Barbara Carey, a pre-school teacher, volunteer basketall coach, and town activist, became co-chairman. The campaign took off.

As it became apparent that certain issues would require special attention and the workload needed to be distributed, Michaud and Carey named coordinators to focus on them. Coordinators were designated to handle such issues as wetlands, water quality, traffic, legal matters, media coverage, volunteer recruitment, business support, petitions, phonathons, fundraising, and consciousness raising (e.g., production of bumper stickers, campaign buttons and fliers). A committed core of about 15 people assumed leadership roles while dozens more helped out with chores as needed.

Turning people out for public hearings was a major strategy. Here, a little bit of foresight exercised by the petition drafters paid off. Besides asking for names and addresses, the petition had requested telephone numbers as well. These now proved invaluable, for they enabled the committee to conduct "phonathons" urging people to attend the hearings and testify. The committee managed to turn out over 800 people for the

52

The petition helped raise public awareness and provided concrete documentation of citizen opposition to the project.

June 15 hearing on the developer's proposed site plan. At the hearing, dozens of people held "STOP Wal-Mart" signs and lined up at the microphone to ask hard questions about the development.

Although the developers didn't need a rezoning, they did need permits, zoning variances, and other approvals. The town had an "open space preservation" ordinance prohibiting commercial development along highways from covering more than 50 percent of a land parcel with impermeable material. Since the developers sought to pave or cover 62 percent of the land, they needed a variance. In addition, because the project was so large, the Massachusetts Environmental Policy Act required an environmental impact report. This revealed that over 200 trees would be razed for the parking lot, that daily car trips in the area would rise by 9,000, and that the development would generate 9,813 gallons of sewage daily to be treated at an on-site septic system.[69]

At the June 15 hearing, residents expressed concerns about traffic, wetlands degradation, water pollution, and air pollution. But mostly they voiced concern over what the development would do to their quality of life.[70] Michaud presented the town planning board with the petition, which by now had acquired over 2,000 signatures.

Wal-Mart's spokesman, Boston lawyer Lawrence Kaplan, was reported in the local paper as commenting after the hearing, "I'm not aware of any precedent where the town can turn you down when you meet all the [development] performance standards. There's no question that we not only meet those standards, we exceed them. Do I feel we'll be approved? Absolutely."[71]

Michaud took a different view. Speaking to a rally of 1,000 people assembled outside before the hearing, she emphasized again that the project was not a done deal: "They need a variety of local permits and approvals, and they have none, I repeat, none. We have a beautiful, friendly little New England town here. Let's keep it that way."[72]

The hearings were important for two reasons. First, they enabled committee members to learn more about the proposed development, information that helped them ask probing questions later and hire relevant expert consultants. Second, the hearings gave citizens a chance to communicate their concerns to public officials.

In mid-July, a public opinion poll conducted on the proposed development rankled Westfordians, who felt it smacked of intimidation. In a telephone survey, pollsters asked residents about their income, educational level, and shopping preferences. The question that people found most offensive was this one:

Are you prepared to support your town officials in an expensive and losing legal battle if [the proposed development] is denied a permit?[73]

Residents also resented a question asking how they felt about the town's receiving $90,000 in annual tax revenues from the project. "I think they're. . . skew[ing] the questions," said Carey. "They asked whether we would like $90,000 in tax revenues. Who would say 'no'? First of all, it's not $90,000; and if they had said it would add 9,000 car trips, it would be a different question."[74]

Another major strategy of the Stop Wal-Mart Committee was generating press coverage. Two local papers had

53

covered the story since April, and this coverage led to wider media interest. In July, a committee member came up with the idea of compiling a special portfolio for the media. The portfolio included letters to the editor and guest editorials against the project that had already been printed in the local paper. Carey and others composed a concise cover letter to accompany the portfolio.

Media coordinator Emily Teller began telephoning local, regional and national media (TV, radio and print) in July. Just as Michaud was new to land-use planning, Teller had little experience in dealing with the press. She caught on quickly. She called producers and editors and told them that since May the Stop Wal-Mart Committee had collected nearly 5,000 signatures in the petition against the superstore and pitched the story as a "David and Goliath" battle. She followed up by mailing the portfolio and the cover letter to anyone interested and called again after the mailing was received.

In making calls, explains Teller, "I tried to go as high as I could. I'd ask for a decisionmaker—the producer, an editor, the bureau chief. I'd say: 'Here's what's going on in my town.'

My assumption was that reporters are always looking for good stories." She also inquired into the newspaper's (or radio or TV network's) process for deciding what stories to cover. In doing so, she found many people eager to help identify key contacts and explain the process. She continued to update her contacts by fax and telephone.

This approach proved effective. The Associated Press ran a small article on Westford. Bigger stories soon followed in *USA Today, The Christian Science Monitor, The Boston Globe, TIME, Newsweek* and other newspapers around the country. Even the *London Times* reported on Westford.[75]

Michaud observed later: "By sending the portfolio to reporters, we in effect did much of their homework. They didn't have to go hunting down facts and stories. The portfolio kind of bootstrapped our media coverage."

On September 16, 1993 *The Wall Street Journal* carried a story headlined "Feisty Yankees Resist Wal-Mart's Drive to Set Up Shop in New England Towns." That same day, Wal-Mart's corporate office in Bentonville, Arkansas, announced its withdrawal from Westford.

The Stop Wal-Mart Committee had won. "Citizen action is great," reflected Emily Teller afterwards. "It really works."

Advice from Elizabeth Michaud

• A committee of motivated volunteers, applying their varied talents strategically, can accomplish miracles.

• Be organized or the paperwork will bury you.

• Circulate a petition. Every name is important. Get phone numbers.

• Turn out everyone you can at public hearings.

• Learn as much as you can about the technical details of the proposed development and be prepared to ask probing questions at public hearings. Think about what in the proposal makes sense and what doesn't.

• Send lots of letters and make lots of phone calls to town officials. They need to know how big the groundswell against the project is.

• Appeal to people's hearts as well as their minds. You need to give people information on technical issues, but you also need to appeal to their love of the town as a place to live, as a place with a close-knit, community feeling.

• It's important not only to have a dedicated committee, but also to meet weekly, to have an agenda for each meeting, and to put people in charge of various aspects of the campaign.

• It's helpful to have an attorney working with you, but it should be a volunteer or pro bono attorney. You can blow a lot of money on a lawyer. [If you live in a small town], don't recruit people who practice law locally, but rather attorneys who live in the community and practice elsewhere. People with local practices in town can't afford to get involved. They are too afraid of alienating in-town clients.

• Have faith that you can succeed. There needs to be one person with a take-charge attitude.

• One person can get the campaign going, if that person bites down on the issue like a bulldog and never lets go. The leader needs to have the attitude that "we're going to do this—no matter what it takes!"

The "community bulletin board" placed on Greenfield's town common for local residents to record their views on a proposed superstore. (Photo: David Molnar, Springfield Union News)

Chapter Nine

Bucking the Establishment:

Greenfield, Massachusetts

What do you do when your local newspaper won't cover your side of the story? When your town council glosses over the downside of a proposed development? When downtown businesses likely to be hurt by superstore sprawl are afraid to speak out for fear of offending customers? All of these problems and more beset citizens in Greenfield, a working-class town of 19,000 in northwestern Massachusetts, in late 1992 and 1993.

Sometime during the summer of 1992, Andree Clearwater learned of Wal-Mart's plans to build a 116,097-square-foot store (slated to expand later to 134,272 feet) and up to two more buildings on the edge of Greenfield. With its 1,372-car parking lot, the total project would equal 264,272 square feet and spread over 63 acres.

Clearwater had managed a shopping mall about 10 years earlier and seen first-hand the damage that outlying commercial centers do to downtowns. "I had already seen the waste that this type of development causes," said Clearwater. "This new project would create major traffic problems. It would hurt the downtown. It would decimate the natural landscape. Their

original plan was to remove the top 28 feet of a ridge overlooking the Connecticut River (which they quickly backed down from after public outcry), opting to 'tuck it into the hillside' where it would be less visible. It was badly designed."

Clearwater began circulating a petition against the project in October 1992. After gathering what she considered a respectable number of signatures, she sent the petition with a letter to the editor of *The Recorder*. The paper printed her letter. Soon thereafter, Clearwater organized a meeting for Greenfield residents who shared her concerns. Fifty people showed up and formed a group called Citizens for Responsible Development (CRD). Phase One of Greenfield's battle against superstore sprawl had gotten under way.

Since the town had previously zoned the proposed development site for industrial purposes and had limited the size of buildings, Wal-Mart and its partner-developer needed to get the land rezoned commercially before building. That was controversial, so the 27-member town council decided to consult the electorate first through a non-binding referendum scheduled for April 6, 1993. Wal-Mart, mean-

while, had been inviting opinion leaders in town to small group meetings in the office of its local attorney.

Between November 1992 and April 1993, CRD concentrated on winning the referendum. It circulated petitions, distributed "Wal-Mart Goodbye" bumper stickers, and spoke out at public hearings. It produced a TV documentary featuring a panel discussion on the proposed development. It increased public awareness. But all the while, CRD members felt frustrated by the reluctance of local business people to speak out. They also felt hobbled by the general perception that the development would go forward no matter what. "The main thing we had to counteract was the feeling of inevitability," says Clearwater.

Meanwhile, several local residents persuaded the town to conduct an independent analysis of the store's fiscal and economic impacts before approving the rezoning. Wal-Mart agreed to pay for the $36,900 study, and the town hired RKG Associates, Inc., a Durham, New Hampshire, firm, to do the research.

The study was supposed to be completed in time to educate the citizenry before the referendum, but it was not actually released until April 2, just four days before the vote—too late for people to read and digest a dry, dense, technical report. The local paper ran an editorial favoring the rezoning and carried a special eight-page supplement on the issue. Conspicuously absent from the supplement, however, was the newly released economic and fiscal impact data. According to the April 6, 1993, *Recorder,* a Wal-Mart-funded group distributed a flier asserting that a "yes" vote would mean the creation of stringent development controls to protect environmental and aesthetic concerns. Without the benefit of the study findings, the voters approved the rezoning by a two-to-one margin.

The referendum itself did not mention Wal-Mart; it simply asked voters:

Shall the zoning bylaws be amended or changed to allow commercial development along the French King Highway?

Although CRD supporters felt many voters probably did not fully understand all the issues involved, they clearly had lost Round One in the battle against sprawl. As of April, most of Greenfield's citizens appeared to want the new superstore...or they were unconcerned about the effects of outlying development.

Soon after the vote, RKG's economic data began to circulate. The report said Wal-Mart would mean a net gain in Greenfield's commercial tax base of $6.9 million and a net increase of 177 jobs over ten years.[76] But it also included some troubling predictions. For example, under a "low-impact" scenario, 91,900 square feet of Greenfield's existing retail space would become vacant as Wal-Mart captured sales from existing merchants. After analyzing and discussing RKG's findings with other economists and retail experts, local business leaders concluded that the new superstore would cause several negative consequences:

• a capture by Wal-Mart of between $15 million and $24 million in existing retail sales, with 65 percent of these sales taken from Greenfield stores (versus stores elsewhere in Franklin County)

• an increase of up to 16,000 car trips per day

• a 33 percent reduction in Greenfield's commercial property values due to increased store vacancies

• an increase of only eight new (lower-paying) jobs after jobs lost through the displacement of existing businesses were taken into account

• the displacement of up to 239,000 square feet[77] of existing retail space in Franklin County (This would result in the vacancy of 65 percent of all retail space devoted to selling department store type merchandise.)

• a net gain of as little as $33,800 in tax revenue (a 1/10 of one percent increase on the annual $24 million town budget)

• a drop in residential property values.[78]

Many Greenfield residents became concerned that the proposed rezoning would leave them with too little space for local industry to grow. They also thought Greenfield didn't need a fourth commercial center, since it already had a struggling downtown, one "dead mall" on the northern end of town and commercial sprawl on the western edge. Why create yet a fourth retail hub, especially one that would further weaken existing centers?

As the minuses for local commerce and sense of community became apparent, so did the need for business leaders to become involved in the debate. Together with other concerned citizens, they formed what would become CRD's successor as the leading superstore opponent: the Greenfield Community Preservation Coalition. Its mission was to sway the town council, which would ultimately have to approve the required rezoning by a two-thirds majority.

Among the Coalition's most prominent players were David L. Bete, Sr., and Kevin O'Neil. Bete is president of Bete Fog Nozzle, which produces industrial spray nozzles and employs 140 people. Bete had voted for the rezoning in April because he thought the downtown didn't offer much and that no one was doing anything to improve it. The new economic data troubled him, however. "We really didn't have enough time in April to digest the RKG report," he said. "What I didn't realize then was that jobs would simply be shifted from one side of town to the Wal-Mart area. The negative impacts suggested by the report were not readily obvious. You had to think about how the proposed development would affect the town, its traffic

patterns, etc." Bete also observed that while the report had assumed only one Wal-Mart store in the Greenfield area, it later became apparent there would be one every 20 miles or so, including at least one other store in Franklin County. Thus Greenfield could not expect to capture sales from the larger region, as the report had suggested.

O'Neil is president of Wilson's Department Store, a downtown retailer. O'Neil had opposed the superstore from the outset but had not played a highly visible role in the debate. It was difficult for him, as it was for other businessmen, to speak out publicly. "Lots of people wanted Wal-Mart," explains O'Neil. "Many businesses were afraid to offend their customers. I finally decided it was too important to stay quiet. The issue affected the entire community."

O'Neil shared others' concerns about the loss of industrial land to large-scale commercial development and about the effects of a fourth commercial center on the three existing ones, but he also saw Greenfield's way of life at stake. "If you want to preserve a town center—with its main street, its courthouse, its shops, insurance agencies and banks—you've got to

The main thing we had to counteract was the feeling of inevitability [about sprawl].
—Andree Clearwater

59

zone your town so these things can remain viable." But O'Neil found little support for this perspective during the first six months of the debate: "Mine was a lonely voice."

Between April and July, 1993 the Coalition worked on persuading the Greenfield planning board and town council to vote against the rezoning, a vote now scheduled for July 21. The Coalition put together and distributed a political advertisement. It also ran several ads. It turned people out for public hearings. Testifying wasn't always easy. In some cases, well-prepared presentations were met with scorn and hostility by local officials.

In the meantime, three pro-business organizations came out publicly against the superstore: the Franklin County Chamber of Commerce, the Greenfield Redevelopment Authority and the Franklin County Community Development Corporation. The support of these pro-development organizations buoyed the spirits of the community preservationists. The momentum seemed now to swing in their favor.

Not for long. On July 21, the town council voted, 19 to 7, for the rezoning.[79] Coalition members felt devastated. Some were so dejected they decided to retreat from the debate altogether. What good would further opposition do?

But Cynthia Heslen, an attorney working with the Coalition, saw the July 21 vote as a setback, not a defeat. Anticipating the outcome, she had done some important research before the vote. She had read Greenfield's town charter and learned that citizens could attempt to overturn the town council's decisions through a general referendum, and had drafted a properly worded petition seeking a referendum that would undo the rezoning. The petition first asked the board to rescind its decision. Failing that, it asked that the issue be put to the voters in the form of a binding referendum. Heslen brought 70 petition forms to the meeting, and after the vote, she gave them to people interested in giving their campaign one more shot. They had seven days to gather the necessary signatures.

Local reporters observed this activity and reported on it afterwards. The town council president, who had favored the rezoning, denounced the petition effort as something that would cost the town money. The local

"If you want to preserve a town center—with its main street, its courthouse, its shops, insurance agencies and banks—you've got to zone your town so these things can remain viable."

—Kevin O'Neil

papor reported him as saying that petition sponsors should "take responsibility for the petitions, so they are accountable for the money they may cost the town."[80] The paper also reported the president as having made statements some people found intimidating: "I have officially asked [organizations opposing the superstore] to make known the names of the coalition members, and they have not seen fit to do so. And this bothers me."

Nonetheless, disheartened Coalition members did nothing with the petition for several days.

Away on vacation during this period, Bete now returned to Greenfield, read the papers and hit the ceiling. "I strongly disagreed with the suggestion that the [superstore] opponents should pay for the referendum. We set public funds aside for referenda. They are part of the democratic process," said Bete. He also observed that the town did not really have to go to the expense of holding a special vote; it could include the rezoning question in the next regular election.

When Ted Wirt, a teacher whose home abutted the Wal-Mart site, called Bete to ask for help gathering petition signatures, Bete said yes.

The following Monday, the local radio reported that Coalition members would be down on the town common on Tuesday to collect petition signatures. Bete recalls the conditions under which this activity took place: "It was pouring rain. We stood under umbrellas and tarps. My pockets were full of water. People were driving up in this downpour to sign these petitions. We asked everybody to call their neighbors." He was impressed by Greenfielders' response: "This was obviously something people felt strongly about. These were people I knew and respected. They cared about their homes and neighborhoods, about the quality of life in Greenfield."

In the middle of this scene, the local cable TV station came down and asked Bete and others to appear on its call-in program: "Guerilla Television." Dripping wet, they went to the station to get their message out to the public.

By Wednesday, Bete and his allies had gathered 600 signatures, 100 more than needed. The town then scheduled the binding referendum vote for October 19. Round Three had begun. It would prove to be the most intensive phase in the entire campaign.

With the vote only eight weeks away, key players in this effort held a small meeting to discuss their next steps. Someone opposed to the superstore suggested they needed a better campaign strategy and recommended Al Norman to organize it.

A Greenfield resident, Norman is a lobbyist for a nonprofit organization that advocates for the elderly. He also has served area politicians as a media consultant. After interviewing Norman, Bete and the other activists hired him to formulate a strategy for winning the October 19 referendum.

Norman thought this assignment required a different approach from that used during the first two phases of the campaign. "I said, 'This is a political campaign, not a campaign to see how much you can educate people about economics. It's our job to appeal to people's hearts as well as minds.'"

Within a week, Norman laid out a comprehensive strategy for winning the October 19 vote. (See p. 33) The campaign against the superstore would be run like a full-fledged political campaign: a media strategy, a grass-roots organizing strategy, radio ads, voter polling, a Get Out The Vote

61

(GOTV) initiative, and poll watching. Norman also developed a timeline with hard deadlines for every task to be completed during the next eight weeks.

One of the first steps suggested by Norman was to give the new group of community organizers a new name. "We had a committee without a name collecting petition signatures," he said. "I suggested we call ourselves the 'We're Against the Wal' Committee." Everyone agreed and named Bete as the new group's chairman.

To give the new campaign visibility and momentum, Norman recommended getting 500 "Stop the Wal" bumper stickers made up and stuck on as many cars by August 30. He also suggested holding a press conference on the town common featuring a traveling "Wal." The committee invited townspeople to come down and record their views on the proposed superstore on a 4' x 6' "community bulletin board." Letters from local residents and citizens in other communities fighting similar battles were tacked onto the "Wal." "We wanted a visible symbol of community opposition to the store," explains Norman. "We took 'The Wal'

down to the town common every Saturday for eight weeks." By the campaign's end, people had filled three walls with letters of opposition. These "Wals" also traveled to Keene, N.H., and Halifax, Mass., where similar coalitions were battling superstores.

Norman also recommended reframing the debate, which until then had focused largely on what the superstore would do to downtown. "Many residents felt negatively toward the downtown and its short-comings," said Norman. "No one would fall on his sword for downtown Greenfield. We needed to shape the issue differently." Norman came up with a variety of ways to communicate one basic theme: Greenfield's small-town way of life was threatened by a superstore. As one of the ads he later produced put it: "There's one thing you can't buy at Wal-Mart: small town quality of life. Once you lose it, you can't get it back." The committee portrayed the electorate's vote on the referendum as a watershed event for the community, not just a decision about a single store: "We're not gaining a store," their ads said, "We're losing our community!"

The media strategy was another critical element, but this was tough to carry out because the local paper had editorialized twice in favor of the rezoning and had not reported information the committee wanted covered. For example, the committee had prepared an overlay drawing to illustrate visually the superstore's size relative to the downtown. The proposed development exceeded the square footage of the entire central business district and was, as the committee put it, the equivalent of three Fenway Parks (Boston's baseball stadium). But the paper did not print the overlay graphic.

Determined to deliver critical information to the voters, the committee raised money to pay for newspaper ads and radio spots. The committee also produced an ad in the form of a four-page, newsprint tabloid that summarized arguments against the superstore. The local paper included the "Retail News" tabloid, which looked like a real newspaper, as a special insert and distributed it to 6,000 regular newspaper subscribers. Five radio ads were produced, all using local opinion leaders. One radio spot, featuring the voice of a popular local supermarket owner, aired 14 times a day.

The committee also took advantage of "free" newspaper space by urging people to write letters to the editor. Norman's strategy called for getting no fewer than 50 people to submit letters by September 20. This goal was exceeded. The committee then copied and redistributed the letters in a packet used to educate people about the issues.

The committee needed to identify its base of voters, so Norman recommended a telephone survey of 1,000 voters to begin on August 23. A Greenfield-owned telemarketing company was hired to assist with a voter opinion poll. The company conducted 4,000 telephone interviews with local voters and produced a list of people for and against the store. The interviews also revealed how individual town precincts would probably vote on the referendum. Lists produced by the interviews proved invaluable the week-end before the referendum, when the volunteer committee members used them to call people leaning against the superstore and remind them to vote.

To show public support one week before the vote, the committee staged a "Main Street New England Walk Against Wal-Mart." A flier announcing this media event urged people to assemble on Main Street to hear speakers from several New England communities—including Westford, Mass.—that had opposed Wal-Mart. "Bring the children, grab a balloon, and walk with us, with our 'Wal' exhibits of letters, through the center of our community," read a promotional flier. "We are proud of the quality of life in our rural town, and we want to see industrial land used as it was intended—not wasted on X, Y, or Z marts. . . Invite your friends to join us!" Steve Alves, a professional filmmaker on the committee, video-taped this march. The tape aired on local cable three times before the vote.

On the day of the referendum itself, the committee "poll-watched." As Norman explains: "You sit by the polling booths all day long and cross names off your list as supporters show up. At 5:00 p.m., with three hours left, you call your supporters who haven't yet voted and ask them to get out and do so."

As it turned out, the GOTV campaign, the poll-watching, the last-minute telephone calls, and the votes of individual citizens all made a difference. On October 19, 1993, voters rejected, by a nine-vote margin, the rezoning of the Wal-Mart site and the proposal to permit commercial stores exceeding 40,000 square feet in Greenfield.

Alves mused later: "The things that affect our daily lives are not well reported. It's hard to understand how community life can change, how relationships that used to be so fluid can be irrevocably altered by large-scale development. We were forced to examine the values of our small-town way of life, and then we voted to preserve them."

64   Postscript: *It was reported a few weeks later that Wal-Mart had spent $30,530 on advertising and other activities aimed at winning the Greenfield referendum, according to campaign finance reports. This was $13,000 more than the "We're Against the Wal" Committee had spent.*[81]

"We were forced to examine the values of our small town way of life, and then we voted to preserve them."

—Steve Alves

Organizing Tips from Greenfield

Al Norman, Political Campaign Consultant

• *It isn't necessarily effective to appeal to people with just facts and figures. Some of that's okay, but you also need to appeal to people's emotions.*

• *Even if you lack zoning hooks, you have the power of public opinion. Large corporations can be very sensitive to this if you are able to get your story covered by the media.*

• *Some consultants recommend that local merchants adjust their product lines and carve out a special niche. That "accommodation" strategy is fine if you've lost the superstore battle. But we did not find that message particularly deep.*

David L. Bete, Sr., President, Bete Fog Nozzle, Inc.

• *Organize quickly.*

• *If possible, tap the expertise of a professional political campaign consultant.*

• *Focus the campaign on the body that will make the key decision. If it's the planning board, focus on the planning board. If it's the town council, focus on the town council. If it's the voters, focus on the voters.*

Cynthia Heslen, Esq., Environmental & Land Use Attorney, Anderson & Kreiger

• *Have an understanding of the big picture. Any large development is likely to need a number of federal, state and local permits or approvals. Prepare a flow chart of those necessary approvals.*

• *Target your efforts and keep fighting.*

• *Remember: even though you may lose a vote before one permitting authority, you could win the next round.*

The city of Lawrence invested in benches, lampposts, trees and brick sidewalks as part of an overall effort to make its downtown attractive and convenient for pedestrians. (Photo: Landplan Engineering & Norm Stuewe)

Chapter Ten

Fending Off Mall Sprawl with a Downtown Plan:

Lawrence, Kansas

Many people think of local comprehensive plans as boring dust-catchers with little or no practical impact. Many plans do fit that description, but boring or not, plans officially adopted by a local governing body can also have real legal muscle and help fight sprawl. Moreover, the policy statements contained in a plan can either undermine or undergird local citizen efforts to prevent sprawl and strengthen the downtown. This is a lesson Lawrence, Kansas, learned in 1991, when the U. S. Court of Appeals for the 10th Circuit held that a downtown plan's goal of protecting the vitality of the central business district provided a reasonable basis for denying a shopping mall developer's request for a rezoning in the cornfields.

The genesis of this case dates back to 1977, when the city of Lawrence adopted *Plan '95*. This document stated that it was official city policy to promote the central business district as the center of business and civic life for the entire Douglas County region. The city reaffirmed this policy in 1982 when it approved the *Comprehensive Downtown Plan.*

The downtown plan called for channeling 70 percent of all new retail space serving the Lawrence area into the downtown. It said government agencies and professional offices should locate downtown. It said downtown should be a "compact, pedestrian-oriented area so as to enhance communication and personal interaction." It thus discouraged drive-in fast-food outlets, but welcomed sit-down restaurants. It sought to prevent a glut of commercial space by prohibiting public funding for any development "far in excess of reasonable foreseeable market demand." Most importantly, the plan stated:

It shall be the general policy to emphasize and lend support to the Central Business District as the primary regional center and to analyze closely any proposal for the extension of regional, community, strip or spot commercial development in light of potential negative impact on the CBD *area [emphasis added].*

In other words, the city would look askance at future proposals for sprawling, outlying developments that might sap the downtown's economic vitality.

It was only a matter of time before someone tested this policy.

In July 1987, Jacobs, Visconsi & Jacobs (JVJ), a national shopping mall developer, asked the city to rezone 61 acres of prime farmland on the outskirts of Lawrence for a regional shopping center. This rezoning request provoked such widespread citizen interest that the Lawrence-Douglas County Metropolitan Planning Commission had to use a junior high school auditorium for public hearings. Over 400 people showed up—so many, in fact, that the Commission extended the hearing over several weeks.

In April 1988, upon the recommendation of the local planning board, the Lawrence City Commission denied the rezoning. The board had argued that a new regional mall in an outlying area would threaten the downtown's role as the city's retail core, and the city commission agreed. Among other things, the city said the proposed development would:

• stimulate urban sprawl, challenge the downtown as the community's center of activity and devastate downtown retail business;

• jeopardize a major public investment—over $38 million since 1950—already spent to preserve and

The compact and walkable nature of Lawrence's downtown serves an important social function. Here local residents can ask about each other's families and otherwise reinforce community bonds.

(Photo: Norm Stuewe, Landplan Engineering) Below, the "pedestrian hostility" of this scene in North Carolina contrasts sharply with downtown Lawrence's pedestrian friendliness. A young couple must return from a mall

by walking in the road because there are no sidewalks. Little chance here of running into friends. (Photo: Julian Price, City Watch)

68

enhance the downtown as the heart of the community;

• cause the loss of a floodplain and wetlands while diminishing the value of prime farmland through traffic, noise, litter, pollution and glare of lights from the proposed mall;

• not increase employment in the area, as argued, but simply draw jobs away from the downtown, forcing lower-income people in city neighborhoods to commute to Lawrence's fringe or give up their employment;

• stimulate the creation of an entirely new "satellite community" and generate new pressures on the city to rezone nearby land for fast-food outlets, gas stations, convenience stores and other types of development; and

• require expensive but unplanned capital improvements and services. The community at large would have to provide police and fire protection, ambulance service, code enforcement, health services and schools to serve the new satellite community stimulated by the mall. Pressures would be brought to locate satellite governmental service facilities—e.g., fire stations, branch post offices, recreation centers and parks—in the mall area.

JVJ then sued the city in both federal and state courts. In the federal suit, JVJ alleged that the city had violated the "due process"[82] and "equal protection"[83] provisions of the U. S. Constitution.[84] JVJ said the city treated developers seeking to build in the suburbs differently from those seeking to build in the downtown. It also argued that the city had violated the federal Sherman Act by using the comprehensive plan to protect downtown merchants from competition.

After losing at the district court level, JVJ appealed to the U. S. Court of Appeals for the 10th Circuit. On March 5, 1991, however, the appellate court affirmed the district court ruling.[85]

The district court had dismissed JVJ's equal protection claim. Its reasoning: developers are treated equally because they all are allowed to develop high-density commercial projects in the downtown and all are forbidden to develop such projects at the city's edge. In any event, the court held, the alleged unequal treatment had a rational basis. The appellate court agreed:

We believe the district court correctly concluded that retaining the vitality of the downtown area was a legitimate interest of the city commission. Declining to rezone property in a manner that would threaten the vitality of the downtown retail area is rationally related to that purpose.

Regarding the anti-trust allegation, the appellate court noted that "Federal anti-trust laws do not apply to anti-competitive acts that derive their authority from the state in the exercise of its sovereign powers." Municipal actions are exempt from anti-trust liability if taken pursuant to a "clearly articulated and affirmatively expressed" state policy to "displace competition with regulation or monopoly service." The Lawrence commission's denial of the rezoning "furthered an affirmatively expressed state policy to displace competition among landowners and users with local regulation by zoning and planning," the court held. It then added:

It generally is recognized that the power to zone and rezone necessarily has foreseeable anti-competitive effects.

Regarding due process, the court

". . . retaining the vitality of the downtown area was a legitimate interest of the [Lawrence] city commission. Declining to rezone property in a manner that would threaten the vitality of the downtown retail area is rationally related to that purpose."

—U.S. Court of Appeals for the 10th Circuit

69

Postscript

concluded that JVJ had not been denied due process rights because it did not have a sufficient property interest in the rezoning application to invoke constitutional protections. The developer had also failed to demonstrate that the city's refusal to rezone the land was arbitrary and capricious, ruled the court.[86]

In the end, the appellate court upheld the city's decision to deny the rezoning in large part because it conflicted with downtown revitalization goals in Lawrence's comprehensive plan.[87]

Gerald L. Cooley, the Lawrence attorney representing the city in this case, underscores the importance of local planning: "We could not have won this case had we not had a long-range downtown plan in place."

Since 1991, Lawrence's commitment to the downtown has eroded and the city commission has approved several sprawling superstores that are expected to weaken the downtown over time. That sprawl-type development has since been allowed on the outskirts of Lawrence does not, however, negate the central point of this case study: that officially adopted local comprehensive plans can help a community defend its zoning decisions against assaults by super-sprawl promoters. Of course, in order to do this, the plan must contain strong pro-downtown, pro-preservation policies. Some plans actually promote sprawl (usually unwittingly) and are therefore of little use in this regard.

The aftermath of the 1991 court decisions also underscores two other points:

• The battle against sprawl rarely comes to an end. Eternal vigilance is required.

• Livable-community advocates should work continuously to ensure that good people run for and are elected to public office. Wise public policies can be meaningless if they do not have the support and understanding of those elected to run the government.

Chapter Eleven

Breaking Away from "Formula" Development:

Cambridge, Massachusetts

According to all the rules slavishly followed by many developers and retailers, the Lechmere discount store in the Cambridgeside Galleria in Cambridge, Mass., should have been a flop. Instead, the store has proven a resounding economic success while the Galleria in which it is located has won several awards. Although Cambridge is not a small town like Westford or Greenfield, the negotiating process followed here may be instructive to others.

The CambridgeSide Galleria is a 764,000-square-foot shopping mall in East Cambridge. Besides housing such national chains as The Gap and Banana Republic, it contains Lechmere, a 123,000-square-foot regional superstore. Lechmere sells electronic entertainment goods, appliances, computers, television sets and other home-related products. It is the leading home electronics retailer in New England. The retail industry would consider it a "category killer" because it dominates the market in which it specializes.

The Lechmere store deviates radically from a traditional discounter's formula for success. First, the store is in the city, not at a highway interchange away from town. It is three stories high, not a one-level box, and consumes only 40,000 square feet of land. It has no surface parking. All parking is located either under or above ground or above the store, and there is less than half the amount of parking that national discounters normally require.[88] Moreover, the parking isn't free: customers pay a $1 fee for the first 90 minutes, more for longer stays. The store's exterior walls are not blank and boring, but enhanced with New England brick and ornamentation. A three-level glass entryway announces the store while upper-floor windows break up the building's mass and allow shoppers to gaze outside. Walkways and a shuttle bus linking the mall to nearby neighborhoods and subway stops enable *almost half of the mall's customers to arrive by foot or transit.* The store makes deliveries, since people obviously can't carry heavy items while walking or taking the bus. In short, this mall and its superstore flagrantly violate the discount industry's conventional wisdom—and still make money.

City Vision and Leverage

Three factors worked in favor of a more "community friendly" discount superstore: vision and hard negotiating by city planners; a willingness by the developer and retailer to experiment; and city leverage provided by a zoning change.

The groundwork was laid in 1978, when architect and urban designer Dennis Carlone completed the East Cambridge Riverfront Plan for the city. At the time, East Cambridge's riverfront was an industrial wasteland that the city wanted to turn into a vibrant, people-oriented neighborhood. The 1978 plan spelled out ways to achieve this transformation. Among other actions, it recommended:

• creating a 16-acre open-space system linking green spaces, planned new development, residential neighborhoods and the Charles River to one another;

• encouraging the preservation and reuse of worthwhile older buildings;

• reducing the role of the automobile by encouraging transit use and creating walkways and bikeways; and

• transforming the dilapidated Lechmere Canal into an attractive public space surrounded by restaurants and housing.

CambridgeSide Galleria at Charles Park. Walkways and a shuttle bus linking the mall to nearby neighborhoods and subway stops enable almost half of the customers to arrive by foot or transit. (Photo: Brad Edgerly)

The city bought into this general concept and soon thereafter began to carry out the recommended public improvements with both state and federal assistance. It repaired the canal, upgraded a nearby transit station, and built a public garage to serve new offices and housing then on the drawing boards.

As real estate activity picked up in the mid-1980s, the city decided it needed clearer rules to guide new development and promulgated the "East Cambridge Development Review Process and Guidelines" in June 1985. Written by Carlone and J. Roger Boothe, the city's urban design director, these guidelines seem bold and even exuberant compared to the plodding nature of many local development rules. (See page 75) Their goal was to:

create a functionally diverse and animated urban development, consisting of handsome background buildings that focus on and enrich the public open space system . . . [N]ew structures must be compatible with East Cambridge's historic architecture. The City seeks new buildings that are timeless, subtle, and elegant structures that will always feel comfortable and inviting to the general public...

The city's goal was to reduce the auto's intrusiveness and to encourage the use of nearby transit.

While the guidelines gave developers a clear picture of the design principles the city expected them to follow, they were merely advisory. No one had to follow them if he didn't want to. To give developers an incentive to follow the guidelines, the city did two things. First, it "downzoned" the land in East Cambridge; in other words, the city reduced the allowable height and bulk of new buildings constructed in the area. Next, the city gave back part of what it had just taken away through the downzoning by permitting developers to increase the size of their projects if they complied with the guidelines.

Willingness to Experiment

Lechmere's flagship store had occupied the East Cambridge site for decades. But as new offices and apartment buildings went up around it, the old store with its acres of surface parking seemed an anachronism. When the city moved to acquire land leased by Lechmere, the company hired Arrowstreet, a Somerville, Mass., architectural firm, to plan a way for Lechmere to stay in East Cambridge in a new store. While Carlone and Boothe represented the city's interests in this planning, a

developer, an architect, and a retail expert spoke for the private sector.

The developer was Stephen Karp, chairman and CEO of New England Development (NED), a Newton, Mass., company. Having developed an interest in the city's revitalization plan, Karp acquired the land underneath Lechmere in 1986. The architect was Robert Slattery, president of Arrowstreet, who had worked with Karp in the past. The retail expert was George Scala, then chairman of Lechmere. As a former senior vice-president for the Dayton-Hudson Corporation, which owned Lechmere during the mid-1980s, Scala had gone to Lechmere to help Dayton-Hudson figure out whether to close, sell, or expand the store. Scala and his colleagues successfully reorganized the company and oversaw the relocation and construction of Lechmere's flagship store in East Cambridge.

The negotiations between Lechmere, NED, and Arrowstreet on the one hand and the city planners on the other were not easy.

Parking was an issue. The developer originally wanted 500 more parking spaces for the mall than the city

73

found acceptable. The city's goal was to reduce the auto's intrusiveness and to encourage the use of nearby transit. In the end, Karp agreed to build only three parking spaces per 1,000 square feet of retail space, or about half that normally required by national retailers, and Lechmere ended up with rooftop parking. He also agreed to the city's request to provide a shuttle bus linking the mall to the transit stops.

Store design was an issue. Lechmere preferred a structure with blank exterior walls. From the retailer's perspective, windows meant having to give up valuable wall space for product displays. With the city taking a firm stand and the developer-architect team coming up with feasible architectural schemes, Lechmere ultimately agreed to a brick building with a glass entryway.

The height of the building was an issue. The city wanted a multi-level store—an anathema to discount retailers. According to Scala, "It's harder to control shoplifting and provide management supervision in a multi-level store. There was also some question as to whether customers would find such an arrangement convenient." After conducting a

East Cambridge Design Guidelines

customer survey, Lechmere agreed to a three-level store. By arranging product displays on either side of a "racetrack" that gives floor supervisors a panoramic view of each floor, Lechmere addressed the problems of shoplifting and department supervision.

The mall's relationship to adjoining public spaces was an issue. The city wanted to encourage shoppers to use the greenways and public spaces planned around the mall. The developer feared security problems might arise from such an arrangement.

Over time, the two sides gradually came to understand the importance of each other's position to the project's success and reached compromises. In 1988 Lechmere's flagship reopened, and in 1990, the entire CambridgeSide Galleria, of which Lechmere had become a part, opened.

An Economic Success

Despite the generally poor economy, and despite breaking the rigid rules normally followed by national and regional chains, the CambridgeSide Galleria and Lechmere have proven a resounding economic success. The

• *The City will not support isolated, individual architectural statements that relate only to themselves.*

• *Attractive and inviting connections to and from adjacent neighborhoods are essential. Further, every possible physical amenity that is easily accessible to and inviting for present East Cambridge residents should be provided.*

• *Private development bordering open spaces must provide direct public access to those spaces.*

• *All developments must include walkways linking buildings to the canal, Riverfront Park, and adjacent neighborhoods.*

• *The City will expect numerous lobbies and other entries in any large-scale development projects, rather than one large lobby and one or two entries serving the entire complex.*

• *Every development must include a mixture of uses —e.g., retail, residential, hotel, office, restaurant.*

• *All parking shall be screened to the satisfaction of the City from all public view.*

• *No building element—e.g., air conditioning equipment, ventilators or chimneys—may project beyond the maximum building height allowed, unless camouflaged by an expressive building top. An expressive building roofline celebrates the building's union with the sky and is reminiscent of late 19th and turn of the century architecture.*

• *Projects must relate to human dimensions and provide a sense of intimacy.*

• *Buildings must provide animated silhouettes that enliven views from the open space system, the historic neighborhoods, the Charles River Basin, and the roads through or to East Cambridge.*

• *All new buildings should be mainly faced with New England brick.*

• *New buildings should maximize visibility and transparency (i.e., display windows) through ground floor retail space.*

75

mall is currently fully leased and sales are generally high.

While this store cost more to build, Lechmere considers it financially successful, according to Scala: "The sales per square foot here are very high. They are as good as it gets with the commodities Lechmere sells."

The shuttle service provided to reduce car trips has succeeded beyond anyone's wildest predictions. It carried 343,000 people the first year and Karp expects it to carry a million in 1993. The pedestrian links

between the mall and surrounding neighborhoods are well used. Lechmere, Karp, the city and Cambridge residents seem well-satisfied.

In the meantime, Karp is purchasing a historic building from Sears that he plans to renovate for retail use. He has also redeveloped an old arsenal in Watertown, Mass., and renovated an old industrial park in Worcester, Mass. Both of these adaptive reuse projects include discount stores.

Advice from Cambridge

Stephen Karp, President and CEO of New England Development: *"When we go into a community, we listen carefully to what people want. We try to accommodate their needs, not just ours. We think we build better projects when we do that. Sometimes it is no more expensive to do things of a higher quality than to do them the wrong way."*

J. Roger Boothe, Director of Urban Design, City of Cambridge, Mass: *"Working with chains is difficult. But we had clout because the allowable density for the CambridgeSide site had been reduced through a 'downzoning.' You need leverage, some way of making the community's voice heard. Without it, you might get a pat on the head, a shrub or two, but that's about it."*

Dennis Carlone, Carlone and Associates, Urban Designers, Cambridge, Mass.: *"If a community wants good results from new development, it must prepare guidelines and plans earlier rather than later. If a community waits for development to come along first, it may be too late. Once a precedent has been established for an area, everybody points to it. They say: 'You allowed that there, so why not here?' Get the rules in place as early as possible."*

"Most importantly, there must be a total vision for an entire area or district, not just a single project. Success comes from establishing good urban relationships between individual buildings, public spaces, and adjoining neighborhoods."

George Scala, Retired Chairman & CEO, Lechmere: *"The developer's willingness to be creative was key to the success of our negotiations. He just kept coming back to the table with ways and means of satisfying the city's concerns. He didn't lose his cool. The city's urban designers also deserve credit for standing firm."*

"Historic preservationists need to understand that many older downtown stores are in trouble because their owners are asleep. Downtown merchants often don't work together. If these downtown stores want to survive, they need to get their act together, come up with a vision for their downtown, and form coalitions and partnerships with local government officials before a giant discounter arrives on the scene. Don't wait for the threat to become imminent. Be forward looking."

"The national discounters need to ask themselves whether they are willing to wait a bit longer for their financial returns in order to preserve the validity of the city. Wall Street investment brokers sometimes make this difficult. They often are unwilling to look at the longer term. This is especially true in retailing."

Robert Slattery, President, Arrowstreet, Inc.: *"The architect's challenge is first to understand quite legitimate and often conflicting needs of the merchant, the developer and the community, and then design an affordable project that really works for everyone involved. CambridgeSide was a unique project, involving creative and determined individuals with the authority to act at the highest levels of their organization, but the process can work in many different communities."*

This chess board park, made possible with assistance from Edgar and Elsa Prince, replaced a dilapidated gas station in Holland, Michigan. The park represents one of many efforts by local residents to rejuvenate their downtown. (Photo: Riverview—Greg Holcombe)

Chapter Twelve

Reviving Downtown Main Streets

Lessons from Holland, Michigan

Limiting sprawl is critical to the preservation of many worthwhile things: cities, downtowns, main streets, wetlands, clean air and water, energy supplies, wildlife habitats, a sense of community and civic spirit. It is only part of the challenge, however. Unless sprawl containment activities are coupled with efforts to improve a community's downtown, they are likely to fail in the long run. If communities allow their downtowns to languish with boarded-up buildings and vacancies, they cannot expect people to live in or visit them. If downtown merchants offer poor merchandise selections, uncompetitive prices, dreary window displays, bad service or inconvenient hours, they cannot expect much customer loyalty. Any or all of these problems can cause a downtown to wither, whether superstore sprawl gnaws at the border or not.

The approach taken to downtown revitalization by Holland, Michigan, is instructive.[89]

Holland is an attractive city of about 31,000 people. It sponsors the annual Tulip Time Festival, an event that draws over half a million visitors. Located five miles from Lake Michigan, it is a clean, well-kept community with attractive neighborhoods. For decades, Holland's downtown held dominion over the shopping market for 25 miles around. By the early 1980s, however, Holland faced problems common to many American downtowns: a deteriorating infrastructure, little money for downtown improvements, and, most troubling of all, new competition from suburban development.

These problems came into sharp focus in 1983, when a developer announced plans to build a 450,000-square-foot shopping mall on the outskirts of Holland. Concerned about the effects of more suburban development on the downtown, local business and civic leaders got together and started talking about what they could do. When the State of Michigan invited communities to participate in the National Trust for Historic Preservation's Main Street Program, Holland applied, was selected, and formed the "Mainstreet Holland" project.

Established in 1984, Mainstreet Holland's mission was to create a strong, vibrant downtown. After identifying the downtown's strengths and weaknesses, Mainstreet Holland outlined a development program. The organization acted as an information clearinghouse and provided a forum for the inspiration and exchange of ideas. It also helped downtown property owners rehabilitate their buildings through three programs:[90]

1. Design Assistance. Mainstreet Holland arranged and paid for up to ten hours of assistance from local design firms to help building owners and tenants prepare preliminary designs and cost estimates.

2. Low-Interest Loans. With participation by four local banks, Mainstreet Holland arranged for low-interest loans to help businesses and property owners undertake building and facade renovations.

3. Rebates. In cooperation with the city, Mainstreet Holland organized rebates to property owners of up to $10,000 for interior and exterior building improvements that conformed with the Mainstreet Design Guidelines. The city funded these rebates through Community Development Block Grant funds.[91]

To complement Mainstreet Holland's efforts, the city carried out a $4 million public improvement program known as "Streetscape/Snowmelt."

This included three major elements: downtown beautification, infrastructure improvements, and a "snowmelt" system. Money for these projects came from the city's general fund; downtown property owners, who contributed through a special tax assessment; and a large private donation.

"Streetscape/Snowmelt" improvements got under way in summer 1988 and were completed by November 1988. Overhead utility wires were buried, sewer and gas lines replaced or upgraded. Historic light fixtures were added. Hundreds of trees and thousands of flowers were planted. Period benches were installed, brick sidewalks laid.

As for "Snowmelt," this was basically a "thermal grid" system installed under 250,000 square feet of downtown Holland's principal driving, walking and parking surfaces. Its purpose was to free downtown streets of ice and slush in the wintertime so pedestrians and shoppers could walk around in a clean, dry environment. To bring this about, the city laid a one-inch, heavy-duty plastic pipe every six inches under street surfaces and sidewalk pavers. The pipe carries hot water and melts snow before it freezes.

The idea of building the snowmelt system came from Gordon Van Wylen, a thermodynamics expert who had served as dean of the University of Michigan's College of Engineering before coming to Holland as president of Hope College. "There were two things going for us," explains Dr. Van Wylen. "We have a municipal power plant near downtown from which waste heat in the form of hot water is available. We also learned about a Swedish design of plastic underground piping used in the snowmelt systems of several Swedish towns." Since the city was already planning to dig up Holland's main street for the streetscape improvements, it seemd an opportune time to add Snowmelt. Holland's public works department initially opposed the idea on the ground that it was impractical and too expensive. The city installed the system anyway.

The timing of Streetscape/Snowmelt wasn't exactly perfect. Just as the city tore up the streets, about 600,000 square feet of new retail space opened up in the suburbs with the completion of the Westshore Mall and Manufacturer's Marketplace, a retail outlet mall. The new malls did hurt the downtown. Among other things, Westshore lured away two major

department stores—J. C. Penney's and Steketees—as well as other retailers. But in November 1988, when Streetscape/Snowmelt was completed, people raved about the results. Holland's "new" streetscape improvements invited people to sit and stroll. Downtown retail business began to pick up.

Many people in the private sector helped out as well. Two in particular were Elsa and Edgar Prince. Lifelong residents of Holland, the Princes had established the Prince Corporation in 1965 to manufacture automotive interior products. The company (which patented the lighted visor) has done well and today employs about 3,000 people. The Princes were saddened as they watched Holland's downtown deteriorate in the early 1980s. "More and more buildings were closing," recalls Mrs. Prince. "A prominent landmark with an old clock tower, a lovely building, was going down, down, down. I said to my husband: 'That really grieves me.'" Mr. Prince took the view that when a city loses its downtown, it loses its sense of community. He also felt that inasmuch as the residents of Holland had been good to him, he should give something back. When nobody seemed to be doing much about the

Tower Clock Building and other languishing buildings, Mr. Prince decided to act. He formed a subsidiary, the Lumir Corporation, and helped establish the Riverview Development Limited Partnership and Freedom Village-Holland. All three bodies would prove vital to Holland's revitalization.

The Lumir Corporation, a development company, was charged with developing a strategic plan for the rehabilitation of key downtown buildings and the recruitment of new businesses into the downtown. One of its first steps was to acquire and renovate the former J. C. Penney's and Steketees department stores, as these were considered pivotal structures. A diverse and broad-based recruitment task force and Hope College, a local liberal arts college, assisted Lumir with its recruitment efforts. The task force convened periodically to identify the types of stores people wanted. Hope College helped prepare a questionnaire asking local residents what businesses they would like to see downtown. With this information in hand, Lumir went after new businesses. "We travelled around the state and observed. Where we found businesses that seemed a good fit, we sat down and talked to them. We had a

vision of what we thought would blend," explains Denny Ellens, Lumir's director. "We wanted the downtown to be unique, a place where people call you by your first name and accept your check, so we brought in small, independent businesses." Today several restaurants, a women's specialty store, a men's clothier, and three art galleries occupy buildings in downtown Holland, thanks to Lumir's recruitment efforts. A children's book store has also expanded.

The mission of the Riverview Development Limited Partnership was to acquire and encourage the development of underused land in downtown Holland. One of the projects undertaken by RDLP was the $2 million, 20,000-square-foot Curtis Center, the first Class A office building in downtown. Other land parcels have since been assembled for future projects.

Freedom Village-Holland was formed to build a $28 million, 348-unit elderly housing complex, Freedom Village, on land adjacent to downtown. As Greg Holcombe, an urban planning consultant, explained, people thought downtown housing would enliven the main street, provide a built-in market for retailers, constitute an informal

"We wanted the downtown to be unique, a place where people call you by your first name and accept your check, so we brought in small, independent businesses."
—Denny Ellens

81

A scene from downtown Franklin, Tennessee, which has worked hard to preserve and enhance its Main Street. (Photo: Tennessee Department of Tourism Development)

Chapter Thirteen

Starting a Downtown Revitalization Program

One of the best long-term strategies for combatting sprawl is to revitalize the downtown, the community's traditional center of commercial, cultural, and social activity. Making downtown "the place to be" helps to attract businesses, shoppers, and appropriate development to Main Street.

Sometimes a downtown's problems seem overwhelming to local citizens. By flooding the community with more commercial space than can reasonably be supported and by diluting the downtown's economic vitality, sprawl can add to those problems. Yet downtown's problems are not insurmountable. Rebuilding the historic commercial district's economic strength simply requires persistence, collaboration, and a clear vision of what you hope to achieve.

By identifying the downtown's major problems, then breaking large tasks down into smaller, achievable steps that gradually bring about positive, incremental change, a community can restore the downtown's economic vitality and make downtown an exciting place to shop, conduct business, dine, live, and visit.

A successful downtown revitalization program will usually have these characteristics:

• A clear focus on a historic or traditional commercial district (either a downtown or a neighborhood commercial district)

• Comprehensive and coordinated design, promotion, organization and economic development activities

• Strong support from both the public and private sectors

• Broad-based community involvement and support

• A strong historic preservation ethic and a commitment to preserve the district's historic commercial buildings

• Willingness to take risks and try new approaches

• Trained, professional staff, whose primary function is to coordinate the activities of committed volunteers

• An active and effective board of directors and committees

• An evolving track record of individual and overall successes in preservation-based commercial revitalization

• Ongoing contact, sharing information and affiliation with other local, state and national preservation-based commercial revitalization programs, through correspondence, memberships, volunteer service and conferences.

How should you get started?

Publicize the issue. Talk with community leaders. Hold a community meeting. Put together a slide show illustrating the successes other communities have had in revitalizing their downtowns, and show this to civic groups, school classes, local businesses, and others. Ask the local newspaper to write a series of articles about the downtown and its revitalization efforts.

Recruit participants. The downtown revitalization program must involve groups and individuals throughout the community in order to be successful. Main Street revitalization requires the cooperation and commitment of a broad-based coalition of public- and private-sector groups:

businesses, civic groups, local government, financial institutions, the chamber of commerce, consumers, and many others. It also involves mobilizing a large number of volunteers to implement activities.

Form an organization. Sometimes an existing organization or institution can take on the downtown revitalization initiative. It's usually more effective, though, to create a new organization that focuses exclusively on the revitalization process and that is unhampered by an existing reputation or by the expectations and particular interests of existing members. The new organization should include broad-based community representation.

Identify barriers to downtown development. Ultimately, it should be as easy for a new business to locate downtown as it is to locate out on the strip. Examine your community's planning and land-use policies, financial programs, building codes, and other tools to see if there are regulatory or financial incentives that encourage sprawl instead of downtown development. List other problems affecting the downtown as well.

Develop a realistic, incremental work plan. Articulate what the community wants the downtown to achieve. Develop a written mission statement and three or four major goals. Then identify some high-priority, but achievable activities the organization can do to meet these goals. In the early years, try to include highly visible physical improvements and promotional events. Remember that you can't tackle all the downtown's problems in one year. Some problems may take years to overcome. Take one step at a time.

Measure your progress. Keep track of the amount of money invested in physical improvements and of the number of new jobs created and new businesses that open. Track the downtown's vacancy rate. Count the number of people who take part in promotional activities. Ask downtown businesses to let you know if their sales are increasing. Publicize the progress the downtown revitalization organization is achieving.

Be persistent. Downtown revitalization doesn't happen overnight. It's a gradual, incremental process. As your organization succeeds in mobilizing resources to tackle small problems, it will strengthen its capacity to confront bigger challenges.

This chapter was written by Kennedy Smith, director of the National Trust for Historic Preservation's National Main Street Center.

86

National Main Street Center

To help communities strengthen their downtowns and neighborhood commercial districts, the National Trust for Historic Preservation established the National Main Street Center (NMSC) in 1980. Main Street is a sustainable economic development program that encourages communities to conserve existing resources and to capitalize on their uniqueness. It urges communities to recognize that the features distinguishing them from other towns are economic assets that can provide a competitive edge in a marketplace dominated by monotonous sameness.

The National Trust's Main Street program emphasizes the following four principles:

1. Economic Restructuring. Main Street must have a solid economic foundation. Existing downtown businesses need to sharpen their competitiveness while downtown organizations need to recruit new businesses, institutions, residents and others to diversify the local economic base.

2. Organization. No revitalization effort can succeed without a strong organization to support and guide it. This requires cooperation and consensus among all the important players—bankers, civic groups, government, merchants and individual citizens—to ensure that the downtown benefits from a community-wide vision of the future.

3. Promotion. Every successful entrepreneur understands marketing. To keep investors on board and cash registers ringing, Main Street must beckon visitors with a welcoming image. From simple graphics to sophisticated sales events and community festivals, the Main Street approach emphasizes taking advantage of the district's unique heritage and personality.

4. Design. A critical goal of every Main Street program is to create a friendly, attractive environment that will keep visitors coming back. Signs, storefronts, landscaping, merchandising displays and promotional materials must all work together to encourage people to shop, stroll and linger downtown. In many communities, the design effort must include rehabilitation of commercial architecture, a precious asset that could be lost unless action is taken to counteract the effects of time and neglect. The Main Street approach emphasizes thoughtful design and a commonsense approach to the reuse of buildings to enhance the long-term appeal of the downtown.

More than 850 communities of all sizes in 34 states have worked with the National Main Street Center to rebuild and revitalize their downtowns and neighborhood commercial districts. The Main Street network helps communities learn from one another. Through a monthly newsletter, a telephone assistance service, and a comprehensive information file, the network gives citizens practical, tested information on a wide range of downtown revitalization issues.

For more information, contact the National Main Street Center, National Trust for Historic Preservation, 1785 Massachusetts Ave., N.W., Washington, D. C. 20036. Tel: (202) 673-4000.[93]

87

The Citadel, a retail outlet mall in Commerce, California. This historic building was rehabilitated by the Trammel Crow Company.
(Photo: The Nadel Partnership)

Chapter Fourteen

Better Models from Around the Country

A superstore should not overwhelm the local economy, thereby creating a commercial glut and displacing a disproportionate number of locally owned small businesses.

Despite the many difficulties communities encounter with national chains, there are some examples of these operations showing a willingness, when asked, to develop stores that are more "community friendly." A "community friendly" store includes the following elements:

• *respect for a community's own vision of itself.* Of overriding importance is deference to the community's own vision regarding how it wants to grow, what it wants to look like, and what it wants to preserve. A company with a good-neighbor policy doesn't play hardball or take advantage of a community's economic weakness by pressuring the community into making exceptions to local laws intended to protect places and values people care about.

• *appropriate scale.* A store's size should be appropriate for the community in which the store locates. The store should not overwhelm the local economy, thereby creating a commercial glut and displacing a disproportionate number of existing businesses, especially locally owned small businesses.[94]

• *re-use of existing buildings.* National retailers concerned about the environment are urged to consider that recycling buildings helps to reduce the depletion of natural resources and the carting off of construction debris to landfills. There are thousands of empty and underused buildings in communities around the country that could be rehabilitated and reused for retail space. The federal tax code allows corporations to take a 20 percent tax credit against the costs of rehabilitating historic structures. Some states and municipalities also provide tax or other (e.g., building code or zoning) incentives for commercial renovation projects.

• *downtown location or proximity to existing commercial centers.* Superstores should not trigger the abandonment (or underuse) of existing buildings and infrastructures by creating entirely new commercial hubs that require expensive public services and infrastructures. If a superstore goes downtown, however, *it must be of an appropriate size and design* so that it does not disrupt or jar with existing neighborhoods and small businesses. This will often require downsizing.

• *parking.* By reducing the amount of impermeable asphalt, stores can alleviate environmental problems and improve their appearance. Some stores have agreed to shared parking arrangements with other stores. Others have substituted above-and below-ground parking (or rooftop parking) for surface lots. Although this type of parking is more expensive than surface parking, stores can substantially reduce the amount of parking needed by locating where people can arrive by foot or transit.

• *pedestrian and transit friendliness.* Many, if not most, people will want (or need) to reach the store by car, but the store's location and design should encourage (or at least enable) people to arrive by foot or public transit. Appropriate locations, attractive architecture, display windows, trees, landscaping, walkways, benches, bus shelters, and other features can help make a development more accessible to pedestrians and transit users. The intermingling of different land uses (e.g., housing, retail, restaurant, office) can help communities to reduce car trips. Special attention should be given to pedestrian connections between superstores and adjoining developments. Stores can provide deliveries, as the Lechmere

store in Cambridge does, to accommodate customers who arrive by foot.

• *good design.* The store should relate harmoniously to its surroundings in terms of scale, design and architecture. Some developers and chains have found that well-designed stores enhance customer loyalty and improve community relations.

• *landscaping and tree preservation.* The store should provide appropriate landscaping and tree buffers, particularly if residential neighborhoods are nearby. The unnecessary bulldozing of trees should be avoided.[95]

· *appropriate signage.* Superstores should recognize that many communities are trying to reduce visual blight by limiting the number and size of advertising signs.

In short, superstores should respect local community values. They should be good neighbors. And they should seek to minimize damage to the environment.

Some people might argue that doing all these things would strip the superstores of all their efficiencies, making it impossible for them to deliver

goods at low prices. Yet it must be recognized that some of these "efficiencies" are defacing America while inconveniencing, disrupting, or costing other people and businesses.

Some developers and superstores have actually demonstrated a capacity to build more "community friendly" stores. Examples are discussed below. Although not every one of these examples incorporates all of the good-neighbor elements discussed above, each represents movement in the right direction.

Home Depot in Tulsa

In Tulsa, the Atlanta-based Home Depot Company has agreed to preserve the art deco facade and tower of the city's Warehouse Market, a historic structure built in 1929. The facade will be incorporated into a $10 million, 130,000-square-foot store being built in downtown Tulsa.

At one point in its history, the building housed the Lido Club, where Cab Calloway, Benny Goodman and Duke Ellington performed. It became known as the Warehouse Market in 1938 and operated as a grocery store until 1978, when it began to fall into disrepair. By 1991, the Eastern Oklahoma Chapter of

90

Tulsa's Warehouse Market features a brilliant terra cotta facade with a central tower. Home Depot plans to rehabilitate the facade of this historic landmark and build its new store behind it. (Photo: John David Heckel)

The Target store at the Terra Vista Center in Rancho Cucamonga, Calif. (Photo: Architects Pacifica Ltd., Irvine, Calif.)

the American Institute of Architects had included the building in its annual list of "vacant, vulnerable and irreplaceable" historic sites.

Home Depot's decision to preserve the facade followed public hearings at which local citizens testified on the importance of the Warehouse Market to Tulsa. In September 1993, the company announced plans to move its store to the rear of the site to make the facade's preservation possible.

This decision drew an enthusiastic response from local public officials and business representatives. Tulsa Mayor Susan Savage praised Home Depot's decision to locate in downtown Tulsa as "a strong endorsement of our central business district" and applauded the company's willingness "to keep this important part of Tulsa's history for future generations to enjoy." Downtown Tulsa Unlimited President Jim Norton said the store should help stabilize the downtown area and stimulate needed development.

Some preservationists regret that the entire building will not be preserved and point out that this project does not meet the U.S. Interior Department's rehabilitation guidelines. Others emphasize the importance to historic

The Denver Dry Goods building in Denver. This historic building was renovated by Rose Associates of New York with assistance from the Denver Urban Renewal Authority. It combines retail, housing, and office space and links up with public transit. This project is seen as an alternative to sprawl. (Photo: Jim Lindberg)

preservation of corporate investment in the older city and are heartened by Home Depot's willingness to preserve the historic facade. *(See photo, page 91)*

The Citadel: A Retail Outlet Mall in Commerce, California

Like superstores, retail outlet malls often stand apart from established cities and towns. The "Citadel Outlet Collection" in Commerce, California, deviates from the practice of plunking an outlet center down in the middle of a meadow. In this case the Dallas-based Trammell Crow Company, one of the nation's largest real estate firms, chose to renovate a historic tire factory on an urban site to house 42 national outlet retailers.

Adolph Schleicher, a tire manufacturer who wanted to convey an image of strength and durability to his products, built the Samson Tire and Rubber Company in 1929 to resemble an Assyrian palace of the 7th century B.C. He hired Los Angeles architects Morgan, Walls and Clement to design a structure a third of a mile long. The building featured a crenellated wall with a six-story temple in the middle as well as bearded warriors and Babylonian princesses carved in bas-relief.

93

The factory produced tires until 1978, when it closed. The building languished until 1983, when the city of Commerce acquired the by-then shabby, boarded-up site. In 1986 the city sponsored a competition inviting developers to adapt the building for new uses.

Working with the Nadel Partnership, a Los Angeles architectural firm, Trammell Crow completed the $118 million project in 1990 and "The Citadel" opened its doors that same year. Today the project accommodates 140,000 square feet of discount retail space, a hotel and conference center, a food court, and 270,000 square feet of office space. The Citadel differs from many outlet malls in several respects:

• It mixes land uses on a single site, thereby reducing the need for car trips from one destination to another.

• It reduces "asphalt blight" by locating the parking in back of the building instead of in front, and by shading the lot with many trees.

• It creates an easily recognized entryway with a broad boulevard of

grey and red interlocking concrete pavers. Palm trees line the concourse.

• It clusters new buildings in back around a series of attractive courtyards.

• It incorporates design elements from the historic palace into the new glass and concrete office buildings located at the rear.

Since opening in 1990, the project has proven financially successful and become a source of local civic pride. A 1993 article in *Value Retail News* cited the Citadel as one of the top ten factory outlet centers in the country. "Our success in attracting nationally recognized tenants such as Ann Taylor, Bass, Eddie Bauer and Geoffrey Beene has enabled the Citadel to increase yearly retail sales despite difficult recessionary conditions," says Tom Bak, senior vice president of Trammell Crow. Retail sales averaged $347 per square foot in 1993. *(See photo, page 88)*

Kmart in Jackson, Wyoming

The Kmart in Jackson, Wyoming, a town of 4,600, shows that a national discounter can design a building that fits in with local architecture and

natural surroundings when pressed to do so. *(See photo, opposite page)*

Local citizens opposed a Kmart store when it was first proposed in 1990. The town initially rejected the project but later narrowly approved it on the condition that Kmart meet certain requirements. Among these were:

• making the building design fit in with Jackson's western rustic architecture;

• providing extra landscaping;

• breaking up the boxiness of the standard Kmart store;

• using more attractive materials for the store's exterior; and

• reducing the size and amount of signage.

Kmart complied with these conditions and built a store generally considered more attractive than its standard box. The developer added clock towers at both ends of the building to reflect a local community landmark and built a porte-cochere in the building's center to give it an easily recognizable entry. He used a combination of masonry and wood for the facade to make the building

The Kmart in Jackson, Wyoming.
(Photo: John K. Grist, Grist Associates,
Inc.)

95

This former U.S. Steel building, listed on the National Register of Historic Places, is expected to be rehabilitated by Price Costco as part of a larger project in downtown Portland, Oregon. (Photo: Hugh Ackroyd)

96

more compatible with local architecture. Instead of installing a loud, garish sign atop a tall pole, Kmart erected a ground-mounted sign that is smaller and less intrusive.

Although Kmart and the developer agreed to reduce the amount of parking, they still put it in front of the building and did not provide much landscaping. The store's location, two miles south of the central business district, also contributes to sprawl. Overall, however, this Kmart shows that a national discounter will build a store that is more compatible with local architecture when the community takes a strong stand.

Lawrence Riverfront Plaza in Lawrence, Kansas

This project illustrates how a retail outlet mall can build up (instead of sprawling over several acres of land), conceal parking areas, and create pedestrian links to the downtown.

The Lawrence Riverfront Plaza, a retail outlet mall, opened on the north end of downtown Lawrence in April 1990. This 150,000-square-foot project includes about 50 stores, including such national chains as Bass, American Tourister, and Van Heusen.

In this case the developer, Chelsea Group of New Jersey, worked with the city to create a project that supports the city's goal of maintaining a strong retail core downtown. The outcome, the Lawrence Riverfront Plaza, is a three-story outlet mall located next to the river in an old industrial area. Although several old, nondescript industrial structures were torn down to make way for this project, one landmark, a historic wire factory, was retained and is slated for rehabilitation. The plaza's architecture is not extraordinary, but the developer and architect did make an effort to reflect the area's manufacturing history and to blend in with the surroundings.

Unlike many outlet malls, this one is not surrounded by acres of asphalt. Instead it is served by a multi-level parking deck. Because the mall is close to Lawrence's main street, people walk from it to the older downtown. Brick walkways provide "safe harbors" for pedestrians, while trees and interesting buildings make the walk from the mall to the downtown more pleasant.

People have responded well to this human-scale project. They like its many amenities—comfortable benches, attractive lighting, and a promenade running the entire length of the building along the river. This lively and interesting plaza is popular and well used.

The Chelsea Group developer receives high marks from the local planning department for having been cooperative and sensitive to the wishes of the community.

Other Examples

Wal-Mart in Eden Prairie, Minnesota

Eden Prairie, Minnesota, is a new suburban community that lacks a traditional downtown and is trying to create one. When Wal-Mart came to Eden Prairie, the city asked the discounter to locate in an area designated by the Eden Prairie plan for commercial development. Wal-Mart agreed to do so. Wal-Mart also agreed to modify certain features of its standard formula to allow more trees, planters, walkways, decorative lights, and special brickwork on the building.[96]

Other communities in which Wal-Mart has agreed to change its standard design include Cerritos, California, where the store is made of granite, limestone and glass; and Lompoc, California, where Wal-Mart designed a Mediterranean theme building at the community's request.

Wal-Mart in Carroll, Iowa

When Wal-Mart expressed interest in locating in or near Carroll, Iowa, the city council invited a planning class at Iowa State University to examine the proposed development and advise the city on how to handle it. The class recommended that Wal-Mart locate downtown so the store would strengthen the retail core instead of weakening it by going outside the city. Wal-Mart accepted the downtown location as well as the city's proposal that the company pay half the cost of a new parking lot that everyone, not just Wal-Mart, could use. Since Wal-Mart moved into the downtown, other national retailers have followed. These decisions to locate downtown have strengthened Carroll's economic vitality.[97]

It must be noted, however, that the downtown store is not considered particularly attractive. It is a plain box with a large parking lot.

Target in Rancho Cucamonga, California

Rancho Cucamonga is a city of about 112,000 people located 15 miles west of San Bernardino. Like Eden Prairie, it has not had a traditional downtown but is trying to create one. It's called Terra Vista Town Center.

In this case, the city enacted strong design guidelines to govern new development in the town center and then required developers to follow them. One result is a 101,800-square-foot Target store that is considered more attractive than the chain's typical box. According to Thomas Bond, project manager for the Town Center project and an associate with Architects Pacifica, Ltd., in Irvine, California, the Target includes several innovative features: a pedestrian promenade linking the main store with a garden center at the other end; a small pavillion in the middle of the promenade; trellises, benches, and attractive lighting to encourage people to wander around; and a strong entryway for the store with columns, decorative metal grillwork, and a granite facade.

Taking their cues from a 100-year-old winery located across the street, the architects who designed this store made an effort to incorporate the area's mission-style architecture into the new Target. *(See photo, page 92)*

Target in Pasadena, California

Target moved into an existing, two-level building in downtown Pasadena in March 1994. The new 175,000-square-foot store, Target's largest, occupies a structure built in 1958 for Robinsons, a major department store. Robinsons closed in January 1993, leaving the city with a large "dead" space in its downtown.

Local residents hope that the new Target will help to revitalize the retail district surrounding the historic Pasadena Playhouse. Built in 1924, this internationally known theater closed in 1966 but reopened in 1986.

T.J. Maxx and Filene's Basement in Chicago, Illinois

The One North State Building located at the corner of Madison and State Streets in downtown Chicago was designed near the turn of the century by Holabird and Roche. Although this historic landmark once housed major department stores, it fell vacant during the mid-1980s when retailers abandoned Chicago for the suburbs.

In 1990, the Chicago-based Tucker Companies purchased this 16-story building and completed its renova-

98

tion the following year. In 1991, T.J. Maxx, an off-price retailer, Filene's Basement, and a number of smaller retailers moved into the building's three lower floors while commercial offices occupied space above.

Instead of forcing an automobile-oriented, monolithic development onto the city, the developer made an effort to fit in with the urban fabric. He provided individual store entrances for each of the 16 retailers located on the street level. These tenants enjoy street access through ornamented metal and glass storefronts.

Ninety-four percent of the retail space is occupied and 89 percent of the office space is leased, according to the Urban Land Institute. The smaller retailers report record sales while the T.J. Maxx and Filene's Basement outlets are among the most successful stores in their respective chains. The renovation has since sparked other revitalization projects in the area, including a $125 million renovation by Marshall Field's and a plan by Toys R Us to come downtown.[98]

T.J. Maxx in Denver, Colorado

For nearly 100 years, the Denver Dry Goods Building served as the city's grande dame department store. In 1987, however, its owner, the May Department Store Company, shut the building down to eliminate competition with another store. Fearing the company might demolish the building, the Denver Urban Renewal Authority (DURA) purchased it for $7.5 million in 1988. Despite several redevelopment attempts, the building languished for six years, eventually becoming a littered eyesore.

In a Cinderella story of sorts, a New York-based developer, Jonathan Rose of Rose Associates, came to the rescue in the early 1990s. With DURA's help, he obtained financing and rehabilitated the building for use as retail, office, and housing space.

The 350,000-square-foot mixed-use project opened for business in October 1993. Retail tenants include Media Play, a home entertainment and software outlet, and T.J. Maxx, which occupies 100,000 square feet. Offices occupy 103,200 square feet of upper-floor space while 51 loft apartments take up the balance. Eighty percent of the apartments are classified as "affordable" while the rest rent at market rates. All of the apartments are already rented.

The building's downtown location, coupled with the fact that both Denver's 16th Street shuttle bus and new light rail system make stops here, make the stores accessible to customers without cars. Residential tenants can walk to work, drop their children off at a nearby day-care center, and take advantage of job training, education, and health-care services in the area.

No special parking facilities were provided for this project. The developer simply pointed out to lenders who might otherwise have required parking that 2,000 spaces already existed in various facilities located within three blocks of the building. *(See photo, page 93)*

Federal tax credits available for the rehabilitation of historic structures and for low-income housing were used in this project. The Denver-based Urban Design Group provided architectural services.

Costco in Portland, Oregon

After being rejected by the city of Portland, Oregon, in 1989, Costco went back to the drawing boards and returned with a new plan in 1994. Under the new plan, Costco will incorporate its warehouse club into an old U.S. Steel warehouse and reuse an adjoining 10,000-square-foot brick office building. Built in 1927, both structures are listed on the National Register of Historic Places. Costco's 1989 plan called for the demolition of the entire complex.

By locating in the city, Costco expects to reduce substantially air pollution and energy use. A preliminary transportation analysis indicates that the urban location will enable the Portland region to reduce automobile traffic by more than 500,000 vehicular miles each month.

As this is written, neither the city nor community residents have had an opportunity to review Costco's new proposal. While they may raise other concerns about the project, to the extent that the new plan re-uses existing buildings and reduces automobile trips, it represents steps in the right direction. *(See photo, page 96)*

Ralph's in San Diego, California

Ralph's Grocery Company, a chain with 160 supermarkets, has located a new store in a mixed-use complex known as the Uptown District in San Diego. The complex provides ground-level retail space with offices and apartments on upper floors. All parking is underground rather than in a surface parking lot.

Although it was more expensive to build this store ($41 per square foot vs. the chain-wide average of $35 per square foot) the store has attracted so much pedestrian traffic that the costs have proven worthwhile. According to research conducted by 1000 Friends of Oregon, the Uptown store ranks among the chain's ten top income generators.[99]

Mitigation

Some communities have tried to mitigate the damaging effects of superstore sprawl on their downtowns through various measures—contributions to downtown merchants associations or historic building renovations, landscaping or minor building design improvements, and the like—when more fundamental changes have proven elusive. Mitigation is not the best way to deal with superstore sprawl because it may still result in a type of development that will wreak long-term damage on the community. Mitigation measures are often just half a loaf, or maybe only a few crumbs.

In general, communities that seriously want to protect their distinctive character should insist that superstores and other types of development fit into the local terrain in permanently beneficial ways. When this approach fails or for some reason is not or cannot be tried, mitigation may be a good fallback strategy.

One example of mitigation comes from North Adams, Mass., where the city leadership persuaded Wal-Mart to make some building design and landscaping improvements and to add more trees than usual. Taking the position that this new store, though located on the edge of town, should still contribute to the downtown, the city also secured a $70,000 contribution from Wal-Mart to help pay for the renovation of a historic art deco theatre. A similar contribution of $25,000 was obtained from a new Stop and Shop.

Chapter Fifteen

Resources and Publications

There are a variety of organizations and publications to which citizens can turn for help. Here are some of them.

Organizations

National Trust for Historic Preservation. A Washington-based, national organization with 250,000 members around the country and seven regional offices, the National Trust can help citizens address the problem of sprawl in various ways. Its staff in seven regional offices provide information and technical assistance to local citizens' groups. The regional offices also provide telephone and on-site assistance, information on experts in various fields, and seed money grants. National Trust publications—*Historic Preservation News* and *Historic Preservation* magazine—can publish stories drawing public attention to local controversies. Sometimes a story can attract helpful national media attention and offers of help from unexpected sources. A professional journal, *Historic Preservation Forum*, provides in-depth information on such topics as preservation planning and urban design.

The Trust's Legal Defense Fund can advise local citizens on legal issues. If important legal principles are at stake,

the Trust may file friend-of-the-court briefs or intervene in litigation. New developments in preservation and land-use law are reported regularly in the Trust's *Preservation Law Reporter.* The Trust's Public Policy Department provides information on relevant federal, state and local policies.

The Trust also sponsors annual Preservation Honor Awards to recognize citizen leadership, good corporate development practices, and other initiatives that improve the livability and character of communities. An annual list of "America's 11 Most Endangered Historic Places" is published by the National Trust to draw public attention to imminently threatened historic sites and buildings. The publicity that surrounds this list can help lead to the rescue of endangered places.

The Trust's National Main Street Center offers assessment visits to help communities evaluate the impact of sprawl on a downtown; provides technical assistance ranging from strategic planning to market analysis; publishes a newsletter, Main Street News; offers educational and networking opportunities; and sponsors an annual "National Town Meeting" bringing together hundreds

of downtown revitalization program leaders and others. (See Chapter 13.)

The Trust also sponsors an annual preservation conference every fall. This event, which attracts more than 1,500 preservationists from around the country, offers educational sessions and opportunities to tap the expertise of knowledgeable individuals in numerous fields.

Speeches, articles and publications available from the Trust include:

• "Communities At Risk: The Consequences of Sprawl." Remarks by Richard Moe, President, National Trust for Historic Preservation, at the University of North Carolina-Chapel Hill, School of Journalism and Mass Communications. October 11, 1993. (Available, free, from National Trust Office of Public Affairs)

• Peggy Robin, *Saving the Neighborhood: You Can Fight Developers and Win.* (Washington D. C.: Preservation Press) 428 pp. $16.95.

• Pamela Dwight, ed., *Landmark Yellow Pages.* (Washington, D.C.: Preservation Press, 1993) 406 pp. $19.95.

• Philip Herr, *Saving Place: A Guide and Report Card for Protecting*

Community Character (Washington, D.C.: National Trust for Historic Preservation, 1991)

• Richard J. Roddewig, "Historic Preservation and the Constitution," *Historic Preservation Forum,* July/August 1993.

• Donovan D. Rypkema, "Property Rights/Property Values," *Historic Preservation Forum,* July/August 1993.

• Edward T. McMahon, "Saving Our Sense of Place," *Historic Preservation Forum,* January/February 1991.

• Arthur Frommer, "Historic Preservation and Tourism," *Historic Preservation Forum,* Fall 1988.

• Daniel Carlson, *Literature Review of Community Impacts and Costs of Urban Sprawl.* Critical Issues Fund Report 1993.

• *Information Series* [100]

• Christopher J. Duerksen and Richard J. Roddewig, *Takings Law in Plain English.* 1994.

• Kennedy Lawson Smith, *Revitalizing Downtowns* (National Main Street

Center). 1988 (rev. 1993). 185 pp.

Contact: NTHP, 1785 Massachusetts Ave., N.W., Washington, D. C. 20036. Tel: 202/673-4000. See Appendix B for NTHP regional office addresses.

The Preservation Network: Every state has a state historic preservation office (SHPO) and most states have private nonprofit statewide preservation organizations and/or state Main Street programs. The SHPOs can identify state preservation laws of possible assistance. They can also direct people to state environmental or other agencies knowledgeable about relevant environmental, land-use, growth management or other policies. Finally, the SHPOs can help identify private nonprofit organizations with an interest and expertise in this area. See Appendix B for SHPO and statewide organization addresses.

Preservation Action (P.A.), a nonprofit preservation advocacy organization, also helps citizens track down useful information and knowledgeable experts. Many P.A. board members are experienced grass-roots activists willing to share ideas and strategies. P.A.'s address is 1350 Connecticut Avenue, N.W., Suite 401, Washington, D. C. 20009. Tel: 202/659-0915.

The Environmental Network. Major national environmental organizations can provide information and expertise on clean air, clean water, transportation, wetlands and environmental policies relevant to local sprawl-containment efforts. These organizations, some of which have state or local chapters, are listed in Appendix B. Most states also have nonprofit statewide environmental advocacy organizations. (See Appendix B.) The Washington-based National Growth Management Leadership Project is tied into this network and is another good resource. Address: 915 15th St., N.W., Suite 600, Washington, D. C. 20005. Tel: 202/628-1270.

The Planning Network: The American Planning Association, a nonprofit organization based in Chicago, conducts research into land-use and zoning issues, publishes *Planning* magazine and special technical reports, and distributes videos and slide shows. The APA also has chapters in every state. Resources available from the APA that are relevant to the sprawl issue include:

• *Aesthetics and Land-Use Controls,* by

Christopher J. Duerksen. PAS Report No. 399. 1986. 45 pp. $20.

• *A Design Manual for Conservation and Development*, Robert D. Yaro et al. 1988. (Lincoln Institute of Land Policy) 184 pp. $36.

• *A Survey of Zoning Definitions*. PAS Report No. 421. 36 pp. $24.

• *Conserving Rural Character and Open Space*, a 65-minute VHS video slide show. 1989. Randall Arendt. $100.

• *Takings and Damages*, a videotape by Christopher J. Duerksen. 1990. $39.95.

• *City Beautiful: Zoning for Aesthetics*, a videotape by Christopher J. Duerksen. 1990. $39.95.

• *Contact:* American Planning Association, 1313 E. 60th Street, Chicago, Illinois 60637. Tel: 312/955-9100.

The Small Towns Institute publishes a magazine, *Small Town*, that regularly covers local planning issues. *Small Town* has published a number of thoughtful articles on the effects of locally owned small businesses (vs. chains) on communities, ways to negotiate with superstores, and other relevant topics.

Contact: Small Towns Institute, Box 517, Ellensburg, Washington 98926. Tel: 509/925-1830.

Other Resources

Other articles, speeches, videos and publications that explain problems with sprawl and offer useful insights include:

Rethinking Suburban Sprawl, a videotape by Andres Duany. Available from Andres Duany & Elizabeth Plater-Zyberk, Architects, 1023 Southwest 25th Avenue, Miami, Florida 33135.

James Howard Kunstler, *The Geography of Nowhere*. (New York: Simon & Schuster, 1993) 304 pp.

William H. Whyte, *City: Rediscovering the Center*. (New York: Doubleday, 1988) 386 pp.

Roberta Brandes Gratz, *The Living City*. (Washington D.C.: Preservation Press 2nd ed., 1994) 382 pp.

Michael Mantell et al, *Resource Guide for Creating Successful Communities*. (Washington, D.C., Island Press, 1990) 209 pp.

Michael Mantell et al, *Creating Successful Communities*. (Washington, D. C.: Island Press, 1990) 233 pp.

Peter Calthorpe, *The Next American Metropolis: Ecology, Community, and the American Dream*. (Princeton: Architectural Press, 1993) 175 pp.

Paul Hawken, *The Ecology of Commerce*. (New York: Harper Business/Harper Collins, 1993) 250 pp.

Manon Pavy and Fritz Wagner, "Focusing the Old Downtown on Specialty Retail for Economic Survival: The Transition of Ponchatoula, Louisiana," *Small Town* magazine, Nov.-Dec. 1993. pp. 18-23.

Maritza Pick, *How to Save Your Neighborhood, City, or Town*. (San Francisco: Sierra Club Books, 1993) 213 pp.

Sprawl Busters, an anti-sprawl campaign book (70 pp) and a video of Greenfield's rally against sprawl. (See Chapter Nine) $15. Write Al Norman, 21 Grinnell St., Greenfield, MA 01301.

103

Appendix A

Economic and Fiscal Impact of Superstores and Sprawl

Cited below are highlights from major studies on superstores and sprawl.

"The Impact of Wal-Mart Stores On Other Businesses and Strategies for Co-Existing," by Kenneth E. Stone, Professor of Economics, Iowa State University. Executive Summary. 1993.

Whether a superstore helps or hurts a local economy depends on whether the economy is growing or stagnating. In Iowa, a state with static growth, the following impacts were observed during a five-year period following the opening of a Wal-Mart store:

Most towns with Wal-Mart stores experience an overall increase in retail sales following the opening of a Wal-Mart. However, businesses that sell products sold by Wal-Mart tend to lose sales after a Wal-Mart opens.

Businesses that sell goods or services that Wal-Mart does not sell may experience higher sales because of the "spillover" effect of traffic generated by a Wal-Mart.

If a Wal-Mart store had sales of $20 million and the total sales of the town only increased by $9 million, then existing merchants suffered a total reduction of sales of $11 million.

Small towns (pop. 500 to 5,000) located near a Wal-Mart store tend to suffer economically. Within five years of a Wal-Mart's opening, small towns within a 20-mile radius of the store suffered cumulative net sales reductions of 19.2 percent. Small towns much further away (but still within driving distance) suffered sales reductions of 10.1 percent.

"The Impact of Discount Stores on Small Town America," by Daniel R. Guimond and Meredith Miller. Hammer, Siler, George Associates, Denver. August 1989.

Public concern over the impact of discount stores surfaced in Colorado in 1985 when Wal-Mart announced plans to open more than 20 stores in the state by 1990. The impacts of 10 Wal-Mart stores on small towns with populations ranging from 1,400 to 14,000 were as follows:

Eight of the 10 Colorado towns showed overall retail sales increases ranging from 7 percent to 43 percent following the arrival of Wal-Marts. The average was 15 percent. However, retail sales in the state as a whole showed almost no increase.

Although most communities experienced a net gain in overall sales, the gains occurred at the expense of existing businesses.

Wal-Mart almost invariably displaces businesses that sell general department store type merchandise.

The economic benefits of major discount stores to small towns are often overestimated or at least countered by negative impacts on retail stores in the downtown. It is inappropriate for towns to provide economic incentives to attract these businesses on the promise of higher sales tax revenues or increased employment. Such a strategy amounts to robbing Peter to pay Paul.

"Impacts of Development on DuPage County (Illinois) Property Taxes," a study prepared by DuPage County Development Department for DuPage County Regional Planning Commission. October 9, 1991.

During the 1980s, DuPage County, Illinois, experienced unprecedented commercial growth and development. Between 1982 and 1988, property taxes increased by 85 percent. By 1989, DuPage County homeowners paid the second highest property taxes per capita of all counties in the state. These facts caused the county to reexamine the widely held view that new commercial development helps to keep residential property taxes down.

After studying the relationship between commercial development and property taxes, DuPage County reached these conclusions:

Nonresidential development is a major contributor to property tax increases in DuPage County.

The conventional wisdom is that nonresidential development brings positive tax benefits to local taxing bodies. However, such development may not result in the positive fiscal impacts previously assumed.

Most fiscal impact analyses look only at a limited set of direct impact factors that are easy to predict. They do not examine indirect impacts. They also view fiscal impacts of individual developments in isolation from the impacts of other developments. They thus do not account for spillover effects or cumulative development impacts.

The largest single contributor to personal property tax increases throughout DuPage County is new nonresidential development. Such development has three times the impact on tax levies that residential development has.

Commercial, industrial, and office development create many demands on public services that are more costly than residential demands for services. These include police and fire protection as well as transportation improvements.

Staying Inside the Lines: Urban Growth Boundaries, by V. Gail Easley. Planning Advisory Service Report No. 440, American Planning Association, Chicago. 1992.

Findings: ". . . at least five and one-half square miles of rural land in the United States are converted each day to urban, suburban and other uses."

" . . . if current population and development trends continue, the population of Southeast Michigan will increase by only 6 percent over the next 20 years while there will be a 40% increase in developed land. Virtually all of that growth will occur at the urban fringe."

"Sprawl is simply not fiscally responsible behavior and...not in the public interest."

The Fiscal Impact of Mall Development: More is Often Less, by John R. Mullin, Professor of Urban Planning, University of Mass., and Jeanne H. Armstrong, President, LandUse, Inc., Hadley, Mass. September 14, 1989:

Do malls create traffic problems? Yes, and. . . far beyond the estimates provided by the mall developers. Developers will typically look at the traffic impacts from their standpoint. They will not look at the secondary growth [stimulated by the initial development or at the cumulative effects of growth over a period of time.]

Do malls create strips? Overwhelmingly, yes. Wherever we have worked or undertaken research, a strip has become a by-product of mall development. These strips are rarely programmed against tax revenues. They cause increased traffic, use additional sewer and water capacity and are a blighting influence. When strips are built, the positive fiscal benefit again will decline.

105

Do malls disrupt downtowns? Yes. Typically, department stores are the first to go (and are rarely replaced). They are then followed by national chains with small stores in the Central Business District (CBD). Normally, in a growing area, there will be a decline of 5-10 years in shopping goods sales. Downtowns often come back but their retail base will be smaller, less active and more service oriented. Above all, there is psychological damage: They cease to serve as the heart of the community.

Do malls have fiscal impact well beyond the borders of the community in which they are located? Yes. In some cases they will cause highway systems to be overburdened. In other cases, they will cause a Mom and Pop store to lose patronage and close. These costs are rarely taken into account.

Impact Assessment of the New Jersey Interim State Development and Redevelopment Plan: Executive Summary, by Rutgers University/Center for Urban Policy Research. Principal Investigator: Robert W. Burchell. February 28, 1992.

Findings: This study concluded that, between 1990 and 2010, a New Jersey

106

plan to contain sprawl and channel new investment into traditional urban centers would save New Jersey:

• $1.3 billion in capital infrastructure costs (not counting savings in maintenance and operating costs);

• $400 million in operating costs annually for public school districts and municipalities;

• 36,500 acres of "frail" environmental lands—forests, steep slopes, and critical watersheds;

• 108,000 acres of high-quality farmland;

• water from 4,560 tons of water pollutants from stormwater runoff;

• $740 million in new road costs: $650 million in local road costs and $90 million in state road costs.

• $440 million in water supply and sewer infrastructure costs.

Appendix B

Helpful Contacts

National Trust for
Historic Preservation

Headquarters and Regional Offices

Headquarters
1785 Massachusetts Avenue, NW
Washington, DC 20036
(202) 588-6000

Mid-Atlantic Regional Office
One Penn Center at Suburban Station
Suite 1520
1617 John F. Kennedy Boulevard
Philadelphia, PA 19103
(DE, DC, MD, NJ, PA, VA, WV,
Puerto Rico, Virgin Islands)
(212) 568-8162

Midwest Regional Office
53 W. Jackson Boulevard, Suite 1135
Chicago, IL 60604
(IL, IN, IA, MI, MO, OH, WI)
(312) 939-5547

Mountains/Plains Regional Office
910 Sixteenth Street, Suite 1100
Denver, CO 80202
(CO, KS, MT, NE, ND, OK, SD, WY)
(303) 623-1504

Texas/New Mexico Field Office
500 Main Street, Suite 1030
Forth Worth, TX 76102 *(TX, NM)*
(817) 332-4398

Northeast Regional Office
7 Faneuil Hall Marketplace, 5th Floor
Boston, MA 02109
(CT, ME, MA, NH, NY, RI, VT)
(617) 523-0885

Southern Regional Office
456 King Street
Charleston, SC 29403
(AL, AR, FL, GA, KY, LA, MS, NC, SC, TN)
(803) 722-8552

Western
One Sutter Street, Suite 707
San Francisco, CA 94104
(AK, AZ, CA, HI, ID, NV, OR, UT,
WA, Guam, Micronesia)
(415) 956-0610

State Historic Preservation Officers

Alabama
Alabama Historical Commission
468 South Perry Street
Montgomery, AL 36130-0900
(334) 242-3184

Alaska
Division of Parks,
Office of History & Archeology
3601 "C" Street, Suite 1278
Anchorage, AK 99503-5921
(907) 269-8721

American Samoa
Department of Parks & Recreation
Government of American Samoa
Pago Pago, American Samoa 96799
011-684-699-6914

Arizona
State Historic Preservation Office
Arizona State Parks
1300 West Washington
Phoenix, AZ 85007
(602) 542-4174

Arkansas
Arkansas Historic Preservation
Program
323 Center Street, Suite 1500
Tower Building
Little Rock, AZ 72201
(501) 324-9880

California
Office of Historic Preservation
Department Parks & Recreation
P.O. Box 942896
Sacramento, CA 94296-0001
(916) 653-6624

Colorado
Office of Archeology & Historic
Preservation
Colorado Historical Society
1300 Broadway
Denver, CO 80203
(303) 866-3395

107

Connecticut
Connecticut Historical Commission
59 South Prospect Street
Hartford, CT 06106
(203) 566-3005

Delaware
Delaware State Historic Preservation
Office
15 The Green
Dover, DE 19901
(302) 739-5685

District of Columbia
Historic Preservation Division
614 H Street, NW, Suite 305
Washington, DC 20001
(202) 727-7360

Florida
Division of Historical Resources
Department of State
500 S. Bronough Street
R.A. Gray Building
Tallahassee, FL 32399-0250
(904) 488-1480

Georgia
Office of Historic Preservation
57 Forsyth Street, NW, Suite 500
Atlanta, GA 30303
(404) 656-2840

Guam
Guam Historic Preservation Office
Department of Parks & Recreation
490 Chasan Palasyo
Agana Heights, Guam 96919
011-671-477-9620

Hawaii
State Historic Preservation Division
33 South King Street
6th Floor
Honolulu, HI 96813
(808) 587-0045

Idaho
Idaho State Historical Society
1109 Main Street
Boise, ID 83702-5642
(208) 334-3847

Illinois
Illinois Historic Preservation Agency
1 Old State Capitol Plaza
Springfield, IL 62701-1512
(217) 785-1153

Indiana
Division of Historic Preservation &
Archaeology
402 West Washington Street
Indiana Government Center South
Room W256
Indianapolis, IN 46204
(317) 232-1646

Iowa
State Historical Society of Iowa
Capitol Complex
East 6th & Locust Street
Des Moines, IA 50319
(515) 281-5419

Kansas
Kansas State Historical Society
6425 Southwest 6th Avenue
Topeka, KS 66615-1099
(913) 272-8681

Kentucky
Kentucky Heritage Council
300 Washington Street
Frankfort, KY 40601
(502) 564-7005

Louisiana
Office of Cultural Development
Department of Culture, Recreation
and Tourism
P.O. Box 44247
Baton Rouge, LA 70804
(504) 342-8200

Maine
Maine Historic Preservation
Commission
55 Capitol Street
Station 65
Augusta, ME 04333
(207) 287-2132

Marshall Islands, Republic of the
Secretary of Interior and Outer Island
Affairs
P.O. Box 1454, Majuro Atoll
Republic of the
Marshal Islands 96960
011-692-625-3413

Maryland
Division of Historical & Cultural
Programs
Department of Housing and
Community Development
100 Community Place
3rd Floor
Crownsville, MD 21032-2023
(410) 514-7600

Massachusetts
Massachusetts Historical Commission
220 Morrissey Boulevard
Boston, MA 02125
(617) 727-8470

Michigan
State Historic Preservation Office
Michigan Historical Center
717 West Allegan Street
Lansing, MI 48918
(517) 373-0511

Micronesia, Federated States of
Office of Administrative Service
Div. of Archives & Historic
Preservation
FSM National Government

P.O. Box PS 35
Palikir, Pohnpei, FSM 96941
011-691-320-2343

Minnesota
State Historic Preservation Office
Minnesota Historical Society
345 Kellogg Boulevard West
Level A
St. Paul, MN 55102-1906
(612) 296-5434

Mississippi
Department of Archives & History
P.O. Box 571
Jackson, MS 39205-0571
(601) 359-6940

Missouri
Historic Preservation Program
Division of Parks, Recreation &
Historic Preservation
P.O. Box 176
205 Jefferson
Jefferson City, MO 65102
(573) 751-7858

Montana
State Historic Preservation Office
1410 8th Avenue
P.O. Box 201202
Helena, MT 59620-1202
(406) 444-7715

Nebraska
Nebraska State Historical Society

P.O. Box 82554
Lincoln, NE 68501
(402) 471-4787
Toll Free (800) 833-6747

Nevada
Historic Preservation Office
101 South Steward Street
Capitol Complex
Carson City, NV 89710
(702) 687-6360

New Hampshire
Division of Historical Resources and
State Historic Preservation Office
19 Pillsbury Street
P.O. Box 2043
Concord, NH 03302-2043
(603) 271-6435

New Jersey
Department of Environmental
Protection and Energy
Historic Preservation Office
CN404, 501 East State Street
Trenton, NJ 08625
(609) 984-0176

New Mexico
Historic Preservation Division
Office of Cultural Affairs
Villa Rivera
228 East Palace Avenue
Santa Fe, NM 87503
(505) 827-6320

New York
Parks, Recreation & Historic
Preservation
Empire State Plaza Agency Bldg. #1
Albany, NY 12238
(518) 474-0443

North Carolina
Division of Archives & History
Department of Cultural Resources
109 East Jones Street
Raleigh, NC 27601-2807
(919) 733-4763

North Dakota
State Historical Society of North Dakota
Heritage Center
612 East Boulevard Avenue
Bismarck, ND 58505
(701) 328-2667

Northern Mariana Islands,
Commonwealth of the
Department of Community &
Cultural Affairs
Commonwealth of the North Mariana
Islands
Saipan, Mariana Islands 96950
011-670-664-2120

Ohio
Ohio Historic Preservation Office
Ohio Historical Center
567 E. Hudson Street
Columbus, OH 43211-1030

(614) 297-2600

Oklahoma
State Historic Preservation Office
2704 Villa Prom
Shepherd Mall
Oklahoma City, OK 73107
(405) 521-6249

Oregon
State Parks & Recreation Department
1115 Commercial Street, NE
Salem, OR 97310-1001
(503) 378-5001

Palau, Republic of
Ministry of Community & Cultural
Affairs
P.O. Box 100
Koror, Republic of Palau 96940
011-680-488-2489

Pennsylvania
Bureau of Historic Preservation
Pennsylvania Historical & Museum
Commission
P.O. Box 1026
Harrisburg, PA 17108-1026
(717) 787-4363

Puerto Rico
Office of Historic Preservation
Box 82, La Fortaleza
San Juan, Puerto Rico 00901
(809) 721-2676

Rhode Island
Rhode Island Historical Preservation
Commission
150 Benefit Street
Old State House
Providence, RI 02903
(401) 277-2678

South Carolina
Department of Archives & History
P.O. Box 11669
Columbia, SC 29211
(803) 734-8609

South Dakota
State Historical Preservation Center
900 Governors Drive
Pierre, SD 57069
(605) 773-3458

Tennessee
Department of Environment and
Conservation
401 Church Street
L & C Tower, 21st Floor
Nashville, TN 37243-0435
(615) 532-0109

Texas
Texas Historical Commission
P.O. Box 12276
Austin, TX 78711-2276
(512) 463-6100

Utah
Office of Preservation
Utah State Historical Society
300 Rio Grande
Salt Lake City, UT 84101
(801) 533-3500

Vermont
Vermont Division for Historic
Preservation
135 State Street
4th Floor
Drawer 33
Montpelier, VT 05633-1201
(802) 828-3056

Virgin Islands
Department of Planning &
Natural Resources
Foster Plaza
396-I Anna's Retreat
St. Thomas, USVI00802
(809) 776-8605

Virginia
Department of Historic Resources
Commonwealth of Virginia
221 Governor Street
Richmond, VA 23219
(804) 786-3143

Washington
Office of Archeology & Historic
Preservation
111 21st Avenue, SW

Olympia, WA 98504
(360) 753-4011

West Virginia
West Virginia Division of
Culture & History
Historic Preservation Office
Cultural Center
1900 Kanawha Boulevard East
Charleston, WV 25305-0300
(304) 558-0220

Wisconsin
Historic Preservation Division
State Historical Society of Wisconsin
816 State Street
Madison, WI 53706
(608) 264-6500

Wyoming
Wyoming State Historic Preservation
Office
2301 Central Avenue
4th Floor Barrett Building
Cheyenne, WY 82002
(307) 777-7697

Statewide Preservation
Organizations

Alabama
Alabama Preservation Alliance
P.O. Box 2228
Montgomery, Alabama 36102
(334) 434-7281

Alaska
Alaska Association for Historic
Preservation
645 W. Third Avenue
Anchorage, Alaska 99501-2124
(907) 333-4746

Arizona
Arizona Preservation Foundation
P.O. Box 13492
Phoenix, Arizona 85002
(602) 280-1350

Arkansas
Historic Preservation Alliance of
Arkansas
P.O. Box 305
Little Rock, Arkansas 72203
(501) 372-4757

California
California Preservation Foundation
405 14th Street, Suite 1010
Oakland, California 94612
(510) 763-0972

Colorado
Colorado Preservation, Inc.
910 16th Street, Suite 1100
Denver, CO 80202
(303) 893-4260

Connecticut
Connecticut Trust for Historic
Preservation
940 Whitney Avenue
Hamden, Connecticut 06517-4002
(203) 562-6312

Delaware
Preservation Delaware
Goodstay Center
2600 Pennsylvania Avenue
Wilmington, Delaware 19806
(302) 651-9617

District of Columbia
D.C. Preservation League
1511 K Street, N.W., Suite 739
Washington, D.C. 20005
(202) 737-1519

Florida
Florida Trust for Historic Preservation
P.O. Box 11206
Tallahassee, Florida 32302
(904) 224-8128

Georgia
Georgia Trust for Historic
Preservation
1516 Peachtree Street, N.W.
Atlanta, Georgia 30309
(404) 881-9980

Hawaii
Historic Hawaii Foundation

P.O. Box 1658
Honolulu, Hawaii 96806
(808) 523-2900

Idaho
Idaho Historic Preservation Council
P.O. Box 1495
Boise, Idaho 83701
(208) 386-9124

Illinois
Landmarks Preservation Council
of Illinois
53 West Jackson Boulevard, Suite 752
Chicago, Illinois 60604
(312) 922-1742

Indiana
Historic Landmarks Foundation
of Indiana
340 West Michigan Street
Indianapolis, Indiana 46202-3204
(317) 639-4534

Iowa
Iowa Historic Preservation Alliance
P.O. Box 814
Mount Pleasant, Iowa 52641-0814
(319) 337-3514

Kansas
Kansas Preservation Alliance
P.O. Box 129
Ottawa, KS 66067-0129
(913) 242-9561

Kentucky
Commonwealth Preservation
Advocates, Inc.
P.O. Box 387
Frankfort, Kentucky 40602
(606) 292-2111

Louisiana
Louisiana Preservation Alliance
P.O. Box 1587
Baton Rouge, Louisiana 70821
(504) 928-9304

Maine
Maine Citizens for Historic
Preservation
P.O. Box 1198
Portland, Maine 04104
(207) 775-3652

Maryland
Preservation Maryland
24 West Saratoga Street
Baltimore, Maryland 21201
(410) 685-2886

Massachusetts
Historic Massachusetts, Inc.
45 School Street
Boston, Massachusetts 02108
(617) 723-3383

Michigan
Michigan Historic Preservation
Network
P.O. Box 398
Clarkston, Michigan 48347
(810) 625-8181

Minnesota
Preservation Alliance of Minnesota
275 Market Street, Suite 54
Minneapolis, Minnesota 55405-1621
(612) 338-6763

Mississippi
Mississippi Heritage Trust
P.O. Box 577
Jackson, Mississippi 39205-0577
(601) 354-0200

Missouri
Missouri Alliance for Historic
Preservation
P.O. Box 895
Jefferson City, Missouri 65102
(314) 635-6877

Montana
Montana Preservation Alliance
P.O. Box 1872
Bozeman, Montana 59771-1872
(406) 585-9551

Nebraska
Nebraska Preservation Council, Inc.
2245 A Street

Lincoln, Nebraska 68502
(402) 438-5979

Nevada
(None)

New Hampshire
Inherit New Hampshire, Inc.
P.O. Box 268
Campbell Jenkins Estate
Concord, New Hampshire 03302-0268
(603) 224-2281

New Jersey
Preservation New Jersey, Inc.
The Proprietary House
149 Kearny Avenue, 2nd Floor
Perth Amboy, New Jersey 08861-4700

New Jersey Historic Trust
CN 404, 506-508 East State Street
Trenton, New Jersey 08625
(609) 984-0473

New Mexico
New Mexico Preservation Heritage
Alliance
P.O. Box 2490
Santa Fe, New Mexico 87504-2490
(505) 983-2645

New York
Preservation League of New York
State
44 Central Avenue

Albany, New York 12206-3002
(518) 462-5658

North Carolina
Preservation North Carolina
P.O. Box 27644
Raleigh, North Carolina 27611-7644
(919) 832-3652

North Dakota
Preservation North Dakota
221 Jamestown Mall
Jamestown, North Dakota 58401
(701) 251-1855

Ohio
Ohio Preservation Alliance, Inc.
65 Jefferson Avenue
Columbus, Ohio 43215
(614) 221-0227

Oklahoma
Preservation Oklahoma, Inc.
P.O. Box 25043
Oklahoma City, Oklahoma 73125-0043
(405) 232-5747

Oregon
Historic Preservation League of
Oregon
P.O. Box 40053
Portland, Oregon 97240
(503) 243-1923

Pennsylvania
Preservation Pennsylvania
257 North Street
Harrisburg, Pennsylvania 17101
(717) 234-2310

Rhode Island
(None)

South Carolina
The Palmetto Trust for Historic
Preservation
P.O. Box 12547
Columbia, South Carolina 29211
(803) 771-6132

South Dakota
Historic South Dakota Foundation
P.O. Box 2998
Rapid City, South Dakota 57709
(605) 394-6842

Tennessee
Association for the Preservation of
Tennessee Antiquities
110 Leake Avenue
Nashville, Tennessee 37205
(615) 352-8247

Tennessee Heritage Alliance
Upper Cumberland Institute
Box 5183
Tennessee Tech University
(615) 372-3338

Texas
Preservation Texas, Inc.
c/o Galveston Historical Foundation
2016 Strand
Galveston, Texas 77550
(409) 765-7834

Utah
Utah Heritage Foundation
Memorial House
P.O. Box 28
Salt Lake City, Utah 84110-0028
(801) 533-0858

Vermont
Preservation Trust of Vermont
104 Church Street
Burlington, Vermont 05401
(802) 658-6647

Virgin Islands
St. Croix Landmarks Society
P.O. Box 2855
Frederiksted
St. Croix, Virgin Islands 00840
(809) 772-0598

St. Thomas Historical Trust
28 Havensight
St. Thomas, Virgin Islands 00802
(809) 776-3000

Virginia
Preservation Alliance of Virginia
P.O. Box 1407
Staunton, Virginia 24402-1407
(703) 886-4362

Association for the Preservation of
Virginia Antiquities
204 W. Franklin Street
Richmond, Virginia 23220-5012
(804) 648-1889

Washington
Washington Trust for Historic
Preservation
204 First Avenue, South
Seattle, Washington 98104
(206) 624-7880

West Virginia
Preservation Alliance of West Virginia
P.O. Box 3371
Charleston, West Virginia 25333-3371
(304) 293-3589

Wisconsin
Wisconsin Trust for Historic
Preservation
646 W. Washington Avenue, Suite D
Madison, Wisconsin 53703
(608) 255-0348

Wyoming
(None)

National Growth Management
Leadership Project
Project Coordinating Committee

Alabama
Cahaba River Society
2717 7th Avenue South, Suite 205
Birmingham, AL 35233
(205) 322-5326

California
Greenbelt Alliance
116 New Montgomery, Suite 640
San Francisco, CA 94105
(415) 543-4291

Colorado
Colorado Environmental Coalition
1000 Friends of Colorado
2323 20th Street
Boulder, CO 80304
(303) 443-5931

Florida
1000 Friends of Florida, Inc.
P.O. Box 5948
926 East Park Avenue
Tallahassee, FL 32314
(904) 222-6277

Georgia
The Georgia Conservancy
1776 Peachtree Street, NW
Suite 400 South
Atlanta, GA 30309
(404) 876-2900

Hawaii
Hawaii's Thousand Friends
305 Hahani Street, # 282
Kailua, Hawaii 96734
(808) 262-0682

Illinois
Openlands Project
220 South State Street, #1880
Chicago, IL 60604
(312) 427-4256

Kentucky
Bluegrass Tomorrow
465 E High Street, #208
Lexington, KY 40507-1941
(606) 259-9829

Maine
Natural Resources Council of Main
271 State Street
Augusta, ME 04330
(207) 622-3101

Maryland
Chesapeake Bay Foundation
162 Prince George Street
Annapolis, MD 21401
(410) 268-8816

Massachusetts
1000 Friends of Massachusetts
44 Bromfield Street, Room 615
Boston, MA 02108
(617) 338-6400

Michigan
Michigan Environmental Council
115 W. Allegan, Suite 10B
Lansing, MI 48933-1712
(517) 487-9539

Minnesota
1000 Friends of Minnesota
2200 4th Street
White Bear Lake, MN 55110
(612) 653-0618

Montana
Greater Yellowstone Coalition
P.O. Box 1874
Bozeman, MT 59771
(406) 586-1593

New Jersey
New Jersey Future
204 W State Street
Trenton, NJ 08608
(201) 222-6800

Mr. Sam Hamill
Consultant
146 Carter Road
Princeton, NJ 08540-2103
(609) 393-0008

New Mexico
1000 Friends of New Mexico
823 Gold Street, SW
Albuquerque, NM 87102
(505) 848-8232

115

New York
Regional Plan Association
61 Broadway
11th Floor
New York, NY 10006-2701
(212) 785-8000

North Carolina
Western North Carolina Alliance
P.O. Box 182
Asheville, NC 28802
(704) 258-8737

Ohio
Eco City Cleveland
2841 Scarborough Road
Cleveland Heights, OH 44118
(216) 932-3007

Oregon
1000 Friends of Oregon
534 SW Third Avenue, Suite 300
Portland, OR 97204
(503) 497-1000

Pennsylvania
Pennsylvania Environmental Council
1211 Chestnut Street, Suite 900
Philadelphia, PA 19107
(215) 563-0250

Rhode Island
Save the Bay, Inc.
434 Smith Street

Providence, RI 02908
(401) 272-3540

South Carolina
The South Carolina Coastal
Conservation League
P.O. Box 1765
456 King Street
Charleston, SC 29402
(803) 723-8035

Vermont
Vermont Natural Resources Council
9 Bailey Avenue
Montpelier, VT 05602
(802) 223-2328

Virginia
The Piedmont Environmental Council
P.O. Box 460
45 Horner Street Street
Warrenton, VA 22186
(703) 347-2334

Washington
1000 Friends of Washington
1305 4th Avenue, Suite 303
Seattle, WA 98101
(206) 343-0681

Wisconsin
1000 Friends of Wisconsin
The College of Natural Resources
University of Wisconsin
1900 Franklin Street

Stevens Point, WI 54481
(715) 346-2386

National Environmental
Organizations

Natural Resources Defense Council
1350 New York Avenue, N.W., Suite 300
Washington, D.C. 20005
(202) 783-7800

(NRDC headquarters)
40 West 20th Street
New York, NY 10011
(212) 727-2700

The Wilderness Society
900 17th Street, N.W.
Washington, D.C. 20006-2596
(202) 833-2300

Sierra Club
408 C Street, N.E.
Washington, D.C. 20002
(202) 547-1141

National Wildlife Federation
1400 16th Street, N.W.
Washington, D.C. 20036
(202) 797-6800

National Audubon Society
700 Broadway
New York, NY 10003-9501
(212) 979-3088

End Notes

[1] See "Phase One Report: Retail Sales Impact of Proposed Wal-Mart on Franklin County," by Thomas Muller and Elizabeth Humstone. October 15, 1993. p. 22. See also "Town of St. Albans Zoning Board of Adjustment Conditional Use Approval (Section 413), Application by The St. Albans Group and Wal-Mart Stores for Commercial Retail Development on the Site of Yandow Farm," April 23, 1993. pp. 6, 7, 13, 15, & 21.

[2] See Matt Sutkowski, "Dean: Wal-Mart Willing To Be More Flexible," *Burlington Free Press*, October 22, 1993

[3] See Chris Peck, "CdA on Way to Becoming 'Sprawl-Mart'," *The Spokesman Review*, July 11, 1993, p. A-13.

[4] See Michael de Courcy Hinds, "Despite Many Vacancies, U.S. Is Building Offices," *The New York Times*, February 8, 1993.

[5] Main street widenings proposed for Russellville, Arkansas, and DePere, Wisconsin, offer two of many examples of this phenomenon.

[6] A growing number of communities are revising "auto-centric" zoning codes to encourage the development (or preservation) of more compact, walkable communities. See Peter Calthorpe, *The Next American Metropolis: Ecology, Community, and the American Dream.* (Princeton: Princeton Architectural Press, 1993.)

[7] See Dean Schwanke, "Navigating the Value Retail Marketplace," Urban Land, May 1993, p. 38.

[8] Dec. 31, 1987 letter from Jane Jacobs to Tim McDowell, Director, Economic and Community Development, City of Scranton, Pa. Although Ms. Jacobs refers here to a downtown mall, her point applies to any large influx of commercial development, whether in the form of a mall or a superstore.

[9] $20 million was estimated as the average sum generated by the superstores the previous year.

[10] See Kenneth E. Stone, "Executive Summary: The Impact of Wal-Mart Stores On Other Businesses and Strategies for Co-Existing," 1993. See Appendix A for more details from this study.

[11] See Daniel R. Guimond and Meredith Miller, "The Impact of Discount Stores on Small Town America." Hammer Siler George Associates, Denver. August 1989, pp. 5, 7 and 8.

[12] See Beth Humstone, Jeff Squires, and Thomas Muller, "Fiscal and Economic Impact/Maple Tree Place Mall on Chittenden County Municipalities," July 1989, pp. 10 and 14.

[13] *Ibid.*, pp. 15, 19 and 47.

[14] According to the United Food and Commercial Workers International Union, two superstore companies alone shift $1.011 billion in health care costs annually to other employers. See UFCW news release dated February 22, 1994.

[15] See Donella H. Meadows, "The Global Citizen," November 18, 1993.

[16] The "Policy on Large-Scale Retail Uses" adopted by Vancouver, British Columbia, city council addresses this point. In limiting new retail developments to 10,000 square feet or less, except under certain circumstances, the council stated: "The [development] applicant should demonstrate how the proposed development will improve the *long-term* level of retail competition in the proposed trade area. While recognizing that occupancy by particular firms cannot be guaranteed or enforced, the Council will be more favorably disposed to projects which are likely to permanently increase the number and variety of competing firms in the area. An application which leads to a lessening of competition through increased market concentration in one or a few firms or which can be seen to lead to store closures because of over-saturation of the market will not be viewed positively." See "Reports to Council," Vancouver Planning Dept. Nov. 24, 1987, Appendix A.

[17] For an excellent commentary on this subject, see "The World from Main Street/Caring Businesses Make Good Communities," by Kenneth Munsell. *Small Town* Magazine, March-April 1987, p. 3.

[18] See Marcia D. Lowe, "Reclaiming Cities for People," *World Watch*, July/August 1992.

[19] See Michelle Gregory, "Doing Business with Big Box Retailers," *Zoning News*, Oct. 1993. p. 1

[20] See Jane Seaberry, "For Suburban Youths, Recreation Is No Longer Just Child's Play," *The Washington Post*, May 31, 1993.

[21] "Consumer Expenditures in 1992" (USDL 93-479), U. S. Dept. of Labor, Bureau of Labor Statistics, November 8, 1993.

22 People with an annual income under $10,000 are much more likely than those with higher incomes to travel by walking. See "National Bicycling and Walking Study," Interim Report, Report No. FHWA PD-92-003, Federal Highway Administration, U.S. Dept. of Transportation. November 1991, p. 7.

23 See D'Vera Cohn and Liz Spayd, "D.C. Area Sets Trend for 21st Century," *The Washington Post,* July 28, 1993.

24 See *Monadnock Perspectives,* Vol. 12, No. 1, 1991. Reprint of article by Bryan Rourke of *The Keene (NH) Sentinel.* February 8, 1991.

25 *Ibid.*

26 See Alex Achimore, "Putting the Community Back into Community Retail," *Urban Land* magazine. (Urban Land Institute, Washington, D.C.) August 1993. p. 34

27 See William H. Whyte, *City: Rediscovering the Center.* (New York: Doubleday, 1988) p. 341.

28 See Jim Cory, "Notebook," *Hardware Age.* February 1988, p. 147.

29 Unless otherwise noted, the source of these sidebar statistics is "The Automobile Index," by the Conservation Law Foundation, Boston.

30 For a discussion of disease and fire hazards and landfill problems created by discarded tires, see Tom Arrandale, "Old Tires, New Solutions," *Governing* Magazine. May 1992, p. 22.

31 See Paul Hawken, The Ecology of Commerce (New York: Harper Collins, 1993), p. 85.

32 Source: Energy Information Administration and White House's Climate Change Action Plan. See "Blueprint to Combat Global Warming," *The Washington Post,* October 26, 1993.

33 Oct. 8, 1992 press release of U.S. Dept. of Transportation

34 *Accident Facts,* 1990 edition, published by the National Safety Council. *Hospital Statistics,* 1991 edition, published by the American Hospital Association. Statistics cited in letter by Eugene Stahl, vice president, National Home Life Assurance Company. See also U.S. Dept. of Transportation/ NHTSA press release No. 13-94, April 1, 1994.

35 See October 28, 1992 letter from Peter H. Cross, P.E., to City of St. Albans, Vermont, requesting a water and sewer allocation for "retail development." See also November 16, 1992 minutes of the St. Albans City Planning Commission meeting.

36 E.g., Simi Valley, CA; Lake Placid, NY; Keene, NH; and Greenfield, MA

37 See Chapter 7 for a more complete discussion of the property rights issue.

38 For further guidance concerning appropriate questions to ask, see Philip B. Herr, *Saving Place: A Guide and Report Card for Protecting Community Character.* National Trust for Historic Preservation. Boston. 1991.

39 An example of a court decision upholding a locality's denial of a rezoning because of a comprehensive plan is *Elias* v. *Town of Brookhaven,* 783 F. Supp. 758 (E.D.N.Y. 1992). Here, the U. S. District Court for the Eastern Division of New York stated: "Where zoning is made in accordance with an overall plan it can hardly be the 'spot zoning' that Elias claims."

40 The foregoing discussion describes the way planning and zoning laws work generally. It should be emphasized that there are some differences among the states and that all relevant state laws must be followed.

41 U.S.C. § 4332

42 See Michael Mantell, "State Preservation Law," *A Handbook on Historic Preservation Law,* The Conservation Foundation. 1983. pp. 174-175.

43 See Raymond J. Burby et al, "Is State-Mandated Planning Effective?", Land Use Law. (American Planning Association: Chicago) October 1993, p. 3.

44 *Collins et al v. Land Conservation and Development Commission,* 75 Or App 517 (1985)

45 *Hamilton Downtown Redevelopment Authority* v. *Gravlee,* 602 So. 2d 390 (Ala. 1992)

46 If, like most people, you have little background in state land-use planning and environmental laws, you can start by calling their governor's office to obtain contacts in the state natural resources or environmental protection agencies. (See Appendix B for state historic preservation office contacts.)

47 42 U.S.C. § 4332(2)(C); 40 C.F.R. Part 1500.

48 An example of the use of the Clean Water Act to block a superstore can be found in Keene, N.H., where in October 1992 the U.S. Corps of Engineers denied a developer permission to build a superstore in a wetland and floodplain.

49 16 U.S.C. § 470f; 36 C.F.R. Part 800.

50 49 U.S.C. § 303. Also 49 U.S.C. § 138 (highways) and §2208(b)(5) (airports).

51 See Scott Bernstein, "Imagining Equity: Using ISTEA and the Clean Air Act Amendments," *Environment and Development*, December 1993. American Planning Association: Chicago.

52 Many of these questions were asked by the town of Greenfield, Mass., in evaluating the impact of a proposed superstore. (See Chapter 9 for details)

53 *The Sierra Club Guide to Community Organizing, How to Save Your Neighborhood, City, or Town*, by Maritza Pick, offers additional useful advice on this subject. The guide is available for $12 from the Sierra Club, 730 Polk St., San Francisco, CA 94109. Tel: (415) 776-2211. For helpful tips on fundraising, see L. Peter Edles, Fundraising: Hands-on Tactics for Nonprofit Groups (New York: McGraw-Hill, Inc., 1993).

54 260 U.S. 383 (1922)

55 See *Euclid* v. *Ambler*, 272 U.S. 365 (1926)

56 *The Proceedings of the Government of the United States, in Maintaining the Public Right to the Beach of the Mississippi, Adjacent to New Orleans, against the Intrusion of Edward Livingston*. See *American Law Journal*, John E. Hall. Vol. V (1814), i-xii, 1-91. See also *Thomas Jefferson and the Law*, by Edward Dumbauld.

57 438 U.S. 104, 130 (1978)

58 480 U.S. 470, 488 (1987)

59 783 F. Supp. 758 (E.D.N.Y. 1992)

60 482 U.S. 304 (1987)

61 483 U.S. 825 (1987)

62 483 U.S. at 834

63 112 S. Ct. 2886 (1992)

64 113 S. Ct. 2264 (1993)

65 See Donovan D. Rypkema, "Property Rights/Property Values," *Historic Preservation Forum* (July/August 1993).

66 480 U.S. 470 at 491 (1987).

67 480 U.S. 470 at 491 n. 21. (1987)

68 See *Westford Eagle*, May 6, 1993, p. 5.

69 See *Westford Eagle*, May 20, 1993.

70 See John Collinge, "Westford Residents Protest Plan to Build Wal-Mart," *The [Lowell, Mass.] Sun*. June 16, 1993.

71 *Ibid*

72 *Ibid*

73 See Kathleen Cordeiro, "Retailer Calls for Opinion," Westford Eagle. July 15, 1993, pp. 1 & 8.

74 *Ibid*

75 In October 1993, ABC's "World News Tonight with Peter Jennings" aired a major segment on the Westford campaign, and in November, National Public Radio's "Talk of the Nation" interviewed Michaud and Teller.

76 See *Fiscal and Economic Impact Assessment of the Proposed Wal-Mart Development*, by Land Use, Inc., of Hadley, Mass., and RKG Associates, Inc., of Durham, N.H. April 2, 1993.

77 This displacement would occur under a "high-impact" scenario.

78 Source: Campaign materials provided by the "We're Against the Wal Committee"

79 In June, the Greenfield planning board had approved the rezoning request and recommended its approval to the town council.

80 See July 24, 1993 *The [Greenfield] Recorder*

81 See Ken Willis, "Wal-Mart to Target New Site," *The Recorder*, December 7, 1993.

82 As Brian W. Blaesser and Alan C. Weinstein explain in *Land Use and the Constitution: Principles for Planning Practice* (Planners Press, Chicago, 1989, p. 10): "The term **due process** . . . refers to Constitutional protection given to persons to ensure that laws are not unreasonable, arbitrary or capricious. When such laws affect individuals' lives, liberty, and property, due process requires that

they have sufficient notice and opportunity to be heard in an orderly proceeding suited to the nature of the matter at issue, whether a court of law or a zoning board of appeals. In a word, due process means fairness."

[83] An equal protection violation occurs when government treats similarly situated persons differently for no valid reason.

[84] Under the Fifth Amendment to the U. S. Constitution, no person shall be deprived of property "without due process of law." Under the 14th Amendment, no state shall deprive any person of property "without due process of law; nor deny any person within its jurisdiction the equal protection of the laws."

[85] *Jacobs, Visconsi & Jacobs, Co., et al* v. *City of Lawrence, Kansas,* et al. 927 F 2d 111 (10th Cir. 1991).

[86] *Jacobs, Visconsi & Jacobs v. City of Lawrence, Kansas,* 927 F.2d 111 (10th Cir. 1991). See "Tenth Circuit Upholds Denial of Request to Rezone Property for Suburban Shopping Mall," *Preservation Law Reporter.* 10 PLR 1147-1148. September 1991.

[87] The lawsuit filed by JVJ in state court also alleged due process, equal protection, and other violations of the law, but it, too, was a loser. In a memorandum decision dated April 5, 1991, the District Court of Douglas County, Kansas, echoed the federal court by holding that the goal of retaining the downtown's vitality "constitutes a legitimate concern of the governing body...."

[88] Only three spaces per 1,000 square feet of retail space, instead of the usual five or six (and sometimes seven) spaces.

[89] Leilah Powell, research assistant at the National Trust for Historic Preservation, contributed to this case study.

[90] See Greg Holcombe, "Upper-Floor Housing: An Innovative Approach," *Main Street News*, No. 88, April 1993.

[91] Community Development Block Grant funds come from the U. S. Department of Housing and Urban Development. CDBG funds are available in many communities around the country.

[92] See Greg Holcombe, "Upper-floor Housing: An Innovative Approach," *Main Street News*, No. 88, April 1993.

[93] This chapter was written by Kennedy Smith, director of the National Trust for Historic Preservation's National Main Street Center.

[94] There are, unfortunately, few examples of superstores willing to downsize on their own. Stronger public policies, state as well as local, may be needed in some areas to protect communities against stores so big they overwhelm everything around them.

[95] Sometimes local zoning codes actually encourage such bulldozing through requirements for planter boxes every so many feet. Such codes should be re-examined to permit developers to comply with the code by preserving mature trees whenever possible. An example of a city that has done this is Fairfax City, Virginia.

[96] Eden Prairie later purchased 23 acres across the street from Wal-Mart to give it greater control over future development.

[97] See Jerry Knox, "Dealing with a Volume Chain Store: Carroll, Iowa, Guides Development and Protects Its Downtown," *Small Town* magazine. Ellensburg, Wash. Sept.-Oct. 1991. pp. 19-23.

[98] For more information on this project, see *Project Reference File: One North State*, Vol. 23, No. 4. Jan.-Mar. 1993. (Urban Land Institute: Washington, D. C.)

[99] See "LUTRAQ Update: Making the Land-Use, Transportation, Air Quality Connection." 1000 Friends of Oregon (Portland, Oregon). Vol. 2, No. 1. Jan. 1994. Research conducted by Rebecca Ocken.

[100] The National Trust for Historic Preservation publishes information booklets on various topics—fund-raising, community organizing, preservation techniques, etc. A complete list of topics covered by these booklets is available by writing the Trust.

120